Common Weeds from Iran, Turkey, the Near East and North Africa

Friedrich Bischof

Common Weeds from Iran, Turkey, the Near East and North Africa

Friedrich Bischof

paintings by

Ellen Mostafawy

Eschborn 1978

Published by:

Deutsche Gesellschaft für Technische Zusammenarbeit (GTZ) GmbH
German Agency for Technical Cooperation, Ltd. (GTZ)
Dag-Hammarskjöld-Weg 1, D-6236 Eschborn 1
Federal Republic of Germany

Paintings: E. Mostafawy

Pictures: F. Bischof, W. Koch, K. Petzoldt

Printed by typodruck rossdorf oHG, Bruchwiesenweg 19, D-6101 Rossdorf 1

ISBN 3-88085-061-5

Printed in Germany

Table of contents

	page
Preface	7
Introduction	9
Amaranthaceae	10
Boraginaceae	16
Campanulaceae	18
Caryophyllaceae	20
Chenopodiaceae	30
Compositae	34
Convolvulaceae	64
Cruciferae	70
Cyperaceae	90
Dipsacaceae	92
Euphorbiaceae	94
Gramineae	98
Leguminosae	130
Lythraceae	158
Malvaceae	160
Orobanchaceae	166
Papaveraceae	174
Phytolaccaceae	176
Plantaginaceae	178
Polygonaceae	180
Portulacaceae	182
Primulaceae	184
Ranunculaceae	186
Rosaceae	188
Rubiaceae	190
Scrophulariaceae	194
Solanaceae	196
Umbelliferae	200
Zygophyllaceae	208

Preface

The government-owned Deutsche Gesellschaft für Technische Zusammenarbeit (GTZ) GmbH (German Agency for Technical Cooperation) has been participating for many years in the world-wide efforts to bring about a decisive improvement to the food production in many developing countries.

Crop and post-harvest protection has developed into one of the GTZ's priority activities to this end. While continuing previous activities in this field such as — setting-up and improving crop-protection services, quarantine measures, supplying pesticides and equipment and organising their use — there are increasing demands for programmes to cover weed control, improved application methods, protection for cereal and vegetable crops, promoting subsistence crops and drawing-up publications geared to practical crop protection work.

The present publication contributes towards this latter demand and is meant to assist specialists working on crop-protection, giving them specific information on the problems of recognizing and controlling weeds. The main weeds met in the regions of the Middle East are described and information is given on their range of distributions and how they are to be controlled.

We of course welcome all enquiries from individual countries concerned regarding this publication and plant protection measures in general.

In many regions, the ultimate goal of increasing food production can only be attained through intensified land use. It has been demonstrated in the past that intensive cropping in particular encourages attack by weeds and thus increases weed-control problems.

It is our sincere hope that this brochure may lead to keener recognition of and more pertinent solutions to weed-control problems, so that a further contribution will have been made towards the agricultural development of countries in the Middle East.

GTZ
Section for Crop and Post-Harvest Protection

Introduction

This small study began in 1971 when I was working in Iran and had access to various local libraries and plant collections. The different floras and herbariums were a great help to me but since in weed control the knowledge of seeds and seedlings is of the same importance as that of flowering plants I had to obtain the deficient data by my own research.

However, encouraged by Dr. M. Hille, the Head of the Plant Protection Project of German Technical Aid in Teheran, and technically assisted by Mrs. E. Mostafawy, who provided the watercolour paintings of the seeds and seedlings, I began to gather the necessary material. After my return to Germany I continued my work at the Department of Herbology at the University of Hohenheim, sponsored by Prof. W. Koch. Two additional journeys to North Africa and the Iran were financed by the GTZ (German Agency for Technical Cooperation).

This book is meant as a kind of addenda to the already existing floras. However, I am only too well aware that it covers only a small segment of all the weeds of this area, containing only about one hundred species, and that my listing of the various local names concentrates only on the most striking and important.

For their help in locating the vernacular names, as well as for various corrections, I want to express my thanks to Mr. Termé and Dr. Behdad from Iran, Dr. Günçan und Mr. Dincsoy from Turkey, Dr. Sanad from **Palestine and for the French names to Prof. Petzoldt.**

The synonyms are listed in order to cover the different nomenclatures in use in various countries.

The families and within them the genera and species are arranged in alphabetical order. If not indicated otherwise the scales belonging to the seeds represent one millimetre.

Since the listed weeds are found in various crops and in different regions the references to control measures are kept rather general. In many cases there was no information available at all.

I owe thanks to the GTZ (German Agency for Technical Cooperation) which provided the publication with financial support, and to Prof. W. Koch in whose department at the University of Hohenheim I conducted the time consuming germination tests and where I finished the work.

Khartoum, August 1977   F. Bischof

Alternanthera sessilis (L.) R. Br. **Amaranthaceae**

Synonyms: *Alternanthera achyranthes* Forsk., *Gomphrena sessilis* L., *Illecebrum sessilis* L., *Telanthera amoena* Regel.

Vernacular names:

Farsi:
Arabian: لقمة الغزال (Louqmet el Ghazal)
Turkish: Gazel lokmasi
English: Sessile-flowered globe amaranth
French: Brède chevrette

Similar species: *Alternanthera nodiflora* R. Br.

Habitat: Typical weed in rice-fields and irrigation ditches. South mediterranean plant, Southwest Asia, Iran.

Propagation: Annual to perennial plant, reproduces by seeds, flowering August to January.

Remarks: Controlled by 2,4-D + picloram.

Amaranthaceae

Amaranthaceae

Amaranthus blitoides S. Wats.   **Amaranthaceae**

Synonyms:

Vernacular names:

Farsi:

Arabian:

Turkish:

English: Spreading pigweed, Mat amaranth

French: Amarante fausse blette

Similar species:

Habitat: Growing in fields, orchards and vineyards. Arid areas of the USA, Mexico, Mediterranean countries, Russia, Iran.

Propagation: Annual plant, reproduces by seeds, flowering from May to October.

Remarks: Controlled with 2,4-D, simazine, atrazine, pyrazon, and trifluralin.

Amaranthaceae

Amaranthaceae

Amaranthus retroflexus L.

Amaranthaceae

Synonyms:

Vernacular names:

Farsi: تاج خروس (Tāj khoroos)

Arabian: دلاع (Dillāq)

Turkish: Horoz kuyruğu

English: Pigweed, Redroot

French: Amarante reflechie, Queue de Renard

Similar species: *Amaranthus chlorostachys Willd.*

Habitat: Growing on fertile, gravelly or sandy loam soils with good nitrogen supply up to 1900 m, on cultivated land, along roads and on waste places.
Common throughout the world from tropical to moderate climates.

Propagation: Annual plant, reproduces by seeds, flowering from June to December.

Remarks: Controlled with 2,4-D, simazine, pyrazon, pebulate, and trifluralin.

Amaranthaceae

Boraginaceae

Heliotropium europaeum L.   Boraginaceae

Synonyms:

Vernacular names:

Farsi: آفتاب پرست (Āftāb parast)
اکریر (Akreer)
Arabian: عقربانه ('Agrabanah)
Turkish: Akrep otu
English: European heliotrope, European turnsole
French: Hèliotrop d'Europe

Similar species: *Heliotropium dolosum* de Not.

Habitat: Growing on moist, calcarious loam soils with high nitrogen level in orchards, vineyards and fields.
Mediterranean-submediterranean plant. West Asia, Iran, North Africa, South and West Europe.

Propagation: Annual plant, reproduces by seeds, flowering May to September.

Remarks: Controlled with 2,4-D, pyrazon and urea compounds.

Boraginaceae

Campanulaceae

Legousia falcata Fritsch **Campanulaceae**

Synonyms: *Campanula syriaca* Willd., *Prismatocarpus falcatus* Ten., *Specularia falcata* (Ren.) A. DC.

Vernacular names:

Farsi:

Arabian:

Turkish:

English: Syrian venus'-looking-glass

French: Spèculaire

Similar species: *Legousia speculum-veneris* (L.) Chaix.

Habitat: Growing in cornfields.
Circum-mediterranean plant. Mediterranean countries.

Propagation: Annual plant, reproduces by seeds, flowering April, May.

Remarks: Controlled by 2,4-D.

Campanulaceae

0.2 mm

Caryophyllaceae

Agrostemma githago L. **Caryophyllaceae**

Synonyms: *Githago segetum* Link, *Lychnis githago* Scop.

Vernacular names:

Farsi: سیاه تخمه (Siā tokhmeh)

Arabian: حبة سودا (Habbeh sawdā)

Turkish: Yemlik, Buğday karamuğu

English: Corn cockle

French: Nielle des blés

Similar species: *Agrostemma gracile* Boiss.

Habitat: Growing on fertile, slightly acid, and loamy soils, especially in wheat.
Circum-mediterranean plant, now naturalized in most parts of the world.

Propagation: Annual plant, reproduces by seeds, flowering from April to July.

Remarks: The black seeds are poisonous.
Chemical control with 2,4-D. Since seeds survive in the soil for one year only purification of seeds is a very effective method of control.

Caryophyllaceae

Caryophyllaceae

Cerastium dichotomum L.　　　　　**Caryophyllaceae**

Synonyms:

Vernacular names:

Farsi:

Arabian:

Turkish:

English: Forked mouse-ear

French: Céraiste inflate

Similar species:

Habitat: Growing in cornfields and pastures up to 2000 m.

Mediterranean plant. South and East Europe, North Africa, Southwest Asia.

Propagation: Annual plant, reproduces by seeds, flowering from February to June.

Remarks: Controlled with 2,4-D.

Caryophyllaceae

Silene aegyptiaca (L.) L. f. Caryophyllaceae

Synonyms: *Cucubalus aegyptiaca* L., *Silene atocion* Juss., *Silene orchidea* L.

Vernacular names:

Farsi:

Arabian: أهروان (Ahlawān)

Turkish:

English: Egyptian catchfly

French:

Similar species: *Silene rubella* L.

Habitat:

Propagation: Annual plant, reproduces by seeds, flowering from February to April.

Remarks: Controlled with 2,4-D.

Caryophyllaceae

Caryophyllaceae

Silene conoidea L. **Caryophyllaceae**

Synonyms:

Vernacular names:

Farsi:

Arabian:

Turkish:

English: Conoid catchfly

French: Silene conique

Similar species:

Habitat: Growing in cornfields from 500 to 1800 m.
Turkey, Iran.

Propagation: Annual plant, reproduces by seeds, flowering March to June.

Remarks:

Caryophyllaceae

Vaccaria pyramidata Med.   **Caryophyllaceae**

Synonyms: *Gypsophila vaccaria* Sibth. et Sm., *Saponaria hispanica* Mill., *Saponaria perfoliata* (Gilib.) Hal., *Saponaria segetalis* Neck., *Saponaria vaccaria* L., *Vaccaria hispanica* (Mill.) Rausch., *Vaccaria parviflora* Moench , *Vaccaria segetalis* (Neck.) Garcke

Vernacular names:
Farsi: جغجغک (Jeghjeghak)
Arabian: فول العرب (Foul el Arab)
Turkish: Arap baklası
English: Cowherb, Pink cockle
French: Saponaire des Vaches

Similar species:

Habitat: Growing in cornfields on calcarious soils in continental-submediterranean climate.
South and Central Europe, North Africa, Southwest Asia, North America, Australia, New Zealand, Japan.

Propagation: Annual plant, reproduces by seeds, flowering June to July.

Remarks: Easily controlled with 2,4-D.

Caryophyllaceae

Chenopodiaceae

Chenopodium album L.   **Chenopodiaceae**

Synonyms:

Vernacular names:

Farsi: سلمه تره (Salmeh tareh)
سلمک (Salmak)

Arabian: رکب الجمل (Rokab el Jamel)

Turkish: Ak pazı, Ak kaz ayağı

English: Lamb's quarters

French: Ansérine, Chenopode blanc

Similar species: *Chenopodium hybridum* L., *Chenopodium murale* L., *Chenopodium polyspermum* L.

Habitat: Growing on fertile soils with high nitrogen levels, cultivated land and waste places up to 2000 m.
Eurasia, North Africa, North America.

Propagation: Annual plant, reproduces by seeds, flowering May to October.

Remarks: Plant is very variable in aspect. Young plants often collected as a vegetable.
Controlled by 2,4-D, glyphosate, pyrazon, pebulate, and trifluralin.

Chenopodiaceae

Chenopodiaceae

Salsola kali L.

Synonyms:

Chenopodiaceae

Vernacular names:

Farsi: شوره (Shooreh)

Arabian: اشنان (Eshnān)

Turkish: Dikenli soda otu

English: Russian thistle

French: Soude kali

Similar species:

Habitat: Growing on sandy saline soils, seashores, fields and waste places.
Continental plant. South and Central Europe, North Africa, Asia.

Propagation: Annual to perennial plant, reproduces by seeds, flowering May to October.

Remarks: Controlled with trifluralin.

Chenopodiaceae

Compositae

Achillea santolina L.　　　　　　　　　　　　　　Compositae

Synonyms:

Vernacular names:

Farsi:

Arabian:

Turkish: Servi otu

English: Santolina milfoil

French: Achillée santolin

Similar species:

Habitat: Growing on sandy and gravelly soils in orchards, vineyards and waste places up to 1800 m.
Southwest Asia, Turkey, Iran.

Propagation: Perennial plant, reproduces by seeds and roots, flowering April to June.

Remarks:

Compositae

Acroptilon repens (L.) DC.   **Compositae**

Synonyms: *Centaurea picris* Pall., *Centaurea repens* L. *Acroptilon picris* (Pall.) DC.

Vernacular names:

Farsi: تلخه (Talkheh)
Arabian:
Turkish: Kekre, Acımık
English: Russian knapweed
French: Centaurée aux amères

Similar species:

Habitat: Growing on fertile sandy loam soils in cornfields, pastures orchards, gardens and along ditches up to 1500 m.
Irano-turanian plant. Turkey, Iran, South Russia, USA.

Propagation: Annual plant, reproduces by seeds and leafy shoots from underground stems, flowering June to September.

Remarks: Controlled with 2,4-D.

Compositae

Compositae

Anacyclus clavatus Pers. **Compositae**

Synonyms:

Vernacular names:

Farsi: تاغندست (Tāghendast)
داغندست (Dāghendast)
Arabian: تاغندست (Tāghendast)
Turkish: Dagindest
English: Longwort
French: Anacycle

Similar species: *Anthemis chia* L.

Habitat: Growing in cornfields, roadsides and waste places. North Africa, Southwest Asia.

Propagation: Annual plant, reproduces by seeds, flowering May to October.

Remarks: Killed by early applications of 2,4-D, MCPA + mediben.

Compositae

Calendula arvensis L.   Compositae

Synonyms:

Vernacular names:

Farsi: ميش بهار وحشی (Hamisheh Bahāre vahshee)

Arabian: الحنوة (Alhynawa)

Turkish: Portakal nerkizi, Ayni sefa

English: Field marigold

French: Souci d'Algérie

Similar species: *Calendula aegyptiaca* Desf.

Habitat: Growing on fertile sandy gravelly loamsoils in fields, orange groves and orchards.
Circum-mediterranean plant, North Africa, West Asia, West and Central Europe.

Propagation: Annual plant, reproduces by seeds, flowering throughout the year.

Remarks: Controlled with 2,4-D.

Compositae

Compositae

Centaurea cyanoides Berger. et Wahlenb. **Compositae**

Synonyms:

Vernacular names:

Farsi: گل گندم (Gole Gandom)
Arabian: مرایر (Marayer)
Turkish: Mavi peygamber çiçeği
English: Syrian cornflower
French: Bleuet

Similar species: *Centaurea cyanus* L.

Habitat: Growing on poor soils in cornfields and waste places up to 1700 m.
Southwest Asia.

Propagation: Annual plant, reproduces by seeds.

Remarks: Controlled with 2,4-D.

Compositae

Chondrilla juncea L.

Compositae

Synonyms:

Vernacular names:

Farsi: قندرونک (Qanderoonak)

Arabian: هنباد بري (Hyndibā barri)

Turkish: Ak hindiba

English: Gum succory, Skeleton weed

French:

Similar species:

Habitat: Growing on calcarious, deep and well aerated loam and clay soils in cornfields, vineyards and orchards.
Mediterranean-submediterranean-continental plant.
South and Central Europe to South Russia, Southwest Asia, North Africa, North America, New Zealand, Australia.

Propagation: Perennial plant, reproduces by seeds and roots, flowering July to September.

Remarks: Milky juice used as chewing gum. Only partial control with phenoxy herbicides. Biological control with fungus *Puccinia chondrillina* Bubak et Syd.

45   Compositae

Chrysanthemum coronarium L.   Compositae

Synonyms:

Vernacular names:

Farsi:

Arabian:

Turkish: Krizantem

English: Crown daisy

French: Chrysanthème
des couronnes

Similar species: *Chrysanthemum segetum* L.

Habitat: Growing on rich loamy soils in cornfields, roadsides and waste places.
Circum-mediterranean plant. Europe, mediterranean countries.

Propagation: Annual to biennial plant, reproduces by seeds, flowering February to June.

Remarks: Cultivated as an ornamental.

Compositae

Compositae

Erigeron canadensis L. **Compositae**

Synonyms: *Caenotus canadensis* (L.) Raf., *Conyza canadensis* (L.) Cronqu., *Leptilon canadensis* (L.) Britt.

Vernacular names:

Farsi:

Arabian: حشيشه الجبل (Hasheeshet al Jabel)

Turkish: Şifa otu

English: Horseweed

French: Erigéron du Canada

Similar species: *Erigeron crispus* Pourr.

Habitat: Growing on rich mineral soils in orchards, vineyards, along ditches.
Nearly cosmopolitan in warm and moderate climates.

Propagation: Annual plant, reproduces by seeds, flowering July to August.

Remarks: Controlled with 2,4-D, glyphosate.

49 Compositae

Lactuca orientalis Boiss.

Compositae

Synonyms: *Phenopus orientalis* Boiss.

Vernacular names:

Farsi: شیرتیغی (Shir tighi)

Arabian: باخس (Yakhiss)

Turkish:

English: Oriental lettuce

French: Laitue oriéntale

Similar species:

Habitat: Growing on dry fields, orchards and waste places. Mediterranean-continental plant. Mediterranean countries, Southwest Asia.

Propagation: Perennial shrub, reproduces by seeds, flowering from August to September.

Remarks:

Compositae

Lactuca scariola L.   Compositae

Synonyms: *Lactuca serriola* L.

Vernacular names:

Farsi: گاوچاق کن (Gāv chāq kon)

Arabian: خُس البقر (Khas el Baqar)

Turkish: Yabani salata, Yağ marulu

English: Prickly lettuce, Compass plant

French: Laitue scarole

Similar species: *Lactuca virosa* L.

Habitat: Growing on rich soils, orchards, vineyards, cornfields, waste places.
Submediterranean-eurasian plant. Central and South Europe, West and Southwest Asia, North Africa, North America.

Propagation: Annual or biennial plant, reproduces by seeds, flowering from June to September.

Remarks: Solitary plants place their stem leaves vertically in north-south direction. Poisonous to cattle.
Controlled with 2,4-D.

Compositae

Compositae

Notobasis syriaca (L.) Cass. **Compositae**

Synonyms: *Carduus syriacus* L., *Cirsium syriacum* Gaertn., *Cnicus syriacus* Roth

Vernacular names:

Farsi:

Arabian: غرفـش الجمل (Ghorfush el Jamel)

Turkish:

English: Syrian plumed thistle

French: Chardon de Syrie

Similar species:

Habitat: Growing on rich, loamy soils, fields, roadsides and fallow. Circum-mediterranean plant. Mediterranean countries.

Propagation: Annual plant, reproduces by seeds, flowering from April to July.

Remarks: Controlled by 2,4-D, partly resistant to pyrazon.

Compositae

Silybum marianum (L.) Gaertn.　　　　　　　　**Compositae**

Synonyms: *Carduus marianus* L.

Vernacular names:

Farsi:

Arabian: شوك الجمل　(Shouk el Jamel)

Turkish: Mariam anna dikeni

English: Ladys-thistle

French: Chardon-Marie

Similar species:

Habitat: Growing on stony places, pastures, roadsides, waste places.
Circum-mediterranean plant, Mediterranean countries, Caucasus, Iran.

Propagation: Annual to biennial plant, reproduces by seeds, flowering from April to August.

Remarks: Young leaves are eaten as salad, seeds used for medicinal purposes.
Controlled with 2,4-D, partly resistant to pyrazon.

Compositae

Compositae

Tragopogon buphthalmoides (DC.) Boiss **Compositae**

Synonyms: *Scorzonera buphthalmoides* DC

Vernacular names:

Farsi:

Arabian: ذنب الفرس (Thanab el-Faras)

Turkish: Uskurçina

English: Goats beard, Bulls-eye

French: Salsifis

Similar species:

Habitat: Growing in fields, orchards, vineyards and along roads. East mediterranean plant. Iran, Turkey, Southwest Asia.

Propagation: Perennial plant with strong taproot, reproduces by seeds, flowering April to September.

Remarks:

Compositae

Compositae 60

Xanthium spinosum L. Compositae

Synonyms:

Vernacular names:

Farsi:

Arabian: ٜٜٜٜٜٜٜٜٜٜ (Shubbet)

Turkish: Zincir bıtrağı

English: Spiny cocklebur

French: Lampourde épineuse

Similar species:

Habitat: Growing on rich sandy or gravelly soils with good nitrogen supply on fields and along roads.
Circum-mediterranean plant. Areas with moderate climate in South and North America, South and Central Europe, West Asia, North and South Africa, Australia.

Propagation: Annual plant, reproduces by seeds, flowering July to September.

Remarks:

Compositae

Compositae

Xanthium strumarium L.

Compositae

Synonyms: *Xanthium brasilicum* Vell.

Vernacular names:

Farsi توق (Tooq)

Arabian: شـبيط (Shubbeet)

Turkish: Sıraca otu

English: Cocklebur

French: Lampourde strumarium

Similar species: *Xanthium echinatum* Murr., *X. spinosum* L.

Habitat: Growing on rich loam, clay and sand soils with good nitrogen supply, fields, pastures, roadsides and waste places. Submediterranean-continental plant. South Europe, West Asia to India, North Africa, North America.

Propagation: Annual plant, reproduces by seeds, flowering May to June.

Remarks: Controlled with pyrazon.

Compositae

I

Convolvulus arvensis L.   **Convolvulaceae**
Synonyms: *Convolvulus minor* Gilib.
Vernacular names:
Farsi: لبلاب (Lablāb)
        پیچک (Pichak)

Arabian: عُلیق ('Oleyq)
Turkish: Tarla sarmaşağı
English: Field bindweed
French: Liseron des champs

Similar species: *C. sepium* L.

Habitat: Growing on moist clay and loam soils, fields, gardens and waste places.

Mediterranean-submediterranean plant. Moderate and subtropic areas throughout the world.

Propagation: Perennial plant, reproduces by seeds and roots flowering from May to October.

Remarks: Hard to control because of very far and deep reaching roots.
Controlled with repeated applications of 2,4-D, glyphosate.

Convolvulaceae

Convolvulaceae

Convolvulus pilosellifolius Desr. **Convolvulaceae**

Synonyms:

Vernacular names:
Farsi:

Arabian:

Turkish:

English:

French:

Similar species: *Convolvulus deserti* Hochst et. St.

Habitat: Growing in orchards, irrigated crops and roadsides. Southwest Asia.

Propagation: Perennial plant, reproduces by seeds and roots, flowering April to July.

Remarks:

Convolvulaceae

Convolvulaceae

Cuscuta approximata Bab.   **Convolvulaceae**

Synonyms: *Cuscuta planiflora* Ten. spp. *approximata* (Bab.) Engelm.

Vernacular names:

Farsi: (Ses)

Arabian: (Hamool)

Turkish: Yonka küskütü

English: Dodder

French: Cuscute

Similar species: *Cuscuta planiflora* Ten. and many other *Cuscuta* species.

Habitat: Parasitic plant on *Leguminosae*, especially on alfalfa. East Mediterranean plant, Southwest Asia, Iran.

Propagation: Annual plant, reproduces by seeds and parts of its stem when placed on a host plant, flowering April to October.

Remarks: Best control in the long run is made by purification of the *Leguminosae-seeds*. Small patches in the field are controlled with paraquat. If the whole field is infested, control is made by application of dichlobenil, chlorpropham and chlorthal after cutting the alfalfa. In sugarbeet cycloate is recommended.

Convolvulaceae

Cruciferae

Brassica rapa L. **Cruciferae**

Synonyms: *Brassica campestris* L. var. *rapa* Hartm.

Vernacular names:

Farsi:

Arabian: سولجم (Sooljum)

Turkish: Şalgam

English: Common turnip

French: Chou-rave

Similar species:

Habitat: Growing in cornfields.
Europe, North Africa, Southwest Asia.

Propagation: Annual to perennial plant, reproduces by seeds, flowering March to May.

Remarks: Cultivars grown for various purposes. As a weed probably an escape of cultivated varieties.
Controlled with 2,4-D and pyrazon.

Cruciferae

Cruciferae

Conringia orientalis (L.) Dum.   **Cruciferae**

Synonyms: *Brassica orientalis* L., *Conringia perfoliata* Link, *Erysimum orientalis* Mill., *Erysimum perfoliatum* Crantz

Vernacular names:

Farsi:

Arabian: بجع. (Bajee'a)

Turkish: Doğu koringyası

English: Hares-ear

French: Roquette d'Orient

Similar species:

Habitat: Growing on calcarious, cultivated ground and waste places up to 2000 m.
East-mediterranean-continental plant. South, East and Central Europe, North Africa, Southwest Asia.

Propagation: Annual plant, reproduces by seeds, flowering from February to May.

Remarks: In some areas grown as forage crop.
Controlled with 2,4-D.

Cruciferae

Descurainia sophia Webb.   Cruciferae

Synonyms: *Arabis sophia* Bernh., *Descurea sophia* Schur. *Sisymbrium parviflora* Lam., *Sisymbrium sophia* L., *Sisymbrium tripinnatum* DC., *Sophia vulgaris* Fourn.

Vernacular names:

Farsi: خاکشیر (Khākshir)

Arabian: شـبـت (Sholleek)

Turkish: Uzun süpürge otu

English: Flixweed

French: Herbe de Ste. Sophie
Sisymbre Sophia

Similar species:

Habitat: Growing on sandy soils with good nitrogen supply in cornfields, orchards and waste places from 300 to 1700 m.
Continental plant, Eurasia, Greenland, North Africa, South Africa, North and South America, Australia, New Zealand.

Propagation: Annual-biennial plant, reproduces by seeds, flowering from April to June.

Remarks: Seeds used for medicinal purposes.
Controlled with 2,4-D.

Cruciferae

Cruciferae

Eruca sativa Mill.   Cruciferae

Synonyms: *Brassica eruca* L., *Caulis eruca* E. H. L. Krause, *Crucifera eruca* E. H. L. Krause, *Eruca cappadocica* Reut., *Eruca eruca* Asch. et Graebn., *Eruca foetida* Moench, *Eruca glabrescens* Jord., *Eruca grandiflora* Cav., *Eruca oleracea* St.-Hil., *Eruca rucchetta* Spach, *Eruca sativa* (Hill.) Gars., *Eruca silvestris* Bub., *Eruca vesicaria* ssp., *sativa* Thell., *Euzomum sativum* Link., *Raphanus eruca* Crantz, *Sinapis eruca* Clairv.

Vernacular names:

Farsi: مندرب   (Mandāb)

Arabian: جرجير   (Jarjeer)

Turkish: Bahçe hardalı

English: Garden rocket

French: Roquette

Similar species:

Habitat: Growing on fertile soils up to 1700 m in cornfields and waste places.
Mediterranean plant, West, Central and South Europe, North Africa, Southwest Asia.

Propagation: Annual to biennial plant, reproduces by seeds, flowering from February to June.

Remarks: In some areas grown as vegetable and forage crop. Controlled with 2,4-D, pyrazon.

Cruciferae

Lepidium draba L.   Cruciferae

Synonyms: *Cardaria cochlearia* Spach, *Cardaria draba* (L.) Desv., *Cardiolepsis dentata* Wallr., *Cochlearia draba* L., *Crucifera cardaria* E. H. L. Krause, *Jundzillia draba* Andrz., *Lepidium drabifolium* St. Lager, *Nasturtium draba* Crantz

Vernacular names:

Farsi: ازک (Ozmak)

Arabian: قنبرة (Qāneerah)

Turkish: Kir teresi, Çok senelik yabani tere

English: Hoary cress, Perennial peppergrass

French: Passerage, Pain blanc

Similar species:

Habitat: Growing on cultivated land, especially cornfields, along roads and ditches up to 2000 m.
Mediterranean-continental plant. Europe, Southwest Asia, almost cosmopolitan plant.

Propagation: Perennial plant, reproduces by seeds and roots, flowering April to May.

Remarks: In some areas collected as a vegetable.
Controlled with 2,4-D.

Cruciferae

Cruciferae

Malcolmia africana (L.) R. Br.   **Cruciferae**

Synonyms: *Hesperis africana* L., *Wilckia africana* Halacs.

Vernacular names:

Farsi:
Arabian:
Turkish:
English:
French:

Similar species:

Habitat: Growing on sandy places, in cornfields, roadsides and waste places up to 2800 m.
South Europe, Northwest Africa, Southwest Africa, Iran.

Propagation: Annual plant, reproduces by seeds, flowering from March to April.

Remarks: Controlled with 2,4-D.

Cruciferae

Cruciferae

Moricandia arvensis (L.) DC.   **Cruciferae**

Synonyms:

Vernacular names:

Farsi:

Arabian: كرنب برّى (Kurumb barree)

Turkish: Yabani lahana

English: Cabbage-flowered Moricandia

French: Moricandie des champs

Similar species:

Habitat: Growing in fields and on waste places. Mediterranean countries.

Propagation: Biennial plant, reproduces by seeds, flowering March to June.

Remarks: Controlled with 2,4-D.

Cruciferae

Cruciferae

Myagrum perfoliatum L.   **Cruciferae**

Synonyms:

Vernacular names:

Farsi:

Arabian:

Turkish: Gönül hardalı

English: Gold of pleasure

French: Myagrum perfolié

Similar species:

Habitat: Growing on alkaline sandy soils in cornfields and on roadsides up to 1000 m.
East mediterranean plant. Central and South Europe, West Syria, Caucasia, North Iraq, Central, West and North Iran.

Propagation: Annual plant, reproduces by seeds, flowering April to June.

Remarks: Controlled with 2,4-D and pyrazon.

Cruciferae

Cruciferae

Neslia paniculata (L.) Boiss.   Cruciferae

Synonyms: *Myagrum paniculatum* L., *Neslia apiculata* Fisch et May., *Neslia paniculata* Desv., *Vogelia apiculata* (F. et M.) Vierh., *Vogelia paniculata* (L.) Hornem., *Vogelia sagittata* Med.

Vernacular names:

Farsi:

Arabian: نسليه   (Nislyah)

Turkish:

English: Ball mustard

French: Neslie paniculée

Similar species:

Habitat: Growing on fertile, mostly calcarious and loamy soils, on fields and roadsides.
Continental-submediterranean plant. Europe, North Africa, South Russia, Caucasus, Iran to Tien Shan.

Propagation: Annual plant, reproducing by seeds, flowering from February to May.

Remarks: Controlled with 2,4-D and pyrazon.

Cruciferae

Rapistrum rugosum (L.) All.   Cruciferae

Synonyms: *Myagrum monospermum* Forsk.. *Myagrum rugosum* L.

Vernacular names:

Farsi:

Arabian: خرّاح (Hārrah)

Turkish: Küçük turp

English: Wrinkled gold-of-pleasure

French: Rapistre

Similar species: *Rapistrum perenne* (L.) All.

Habitat: Growing on moist, fertile, calcarious soils in cultivated places, especially grainfields up to 1000 m.
East mediterranean plant. West, Central and South Europe, North Africa, Southwest Asia.

Propagation: Annual plant, reproduces by seeds, flowering from March to May.

Remarks: Controlled with 2,4-D and pyrazon.

Cruciferae

1.25 mm

Cyperaceae

Cyperus rotundus L. **Cyperaceae**

Synonyms: *Chlorocyperus rotundus* Palla, *Cyperus olivaris* Targ.-Tozz., *Pycreus rotundus* Hayek

Vernacular names:
Farsi: اوبارسلام (Oyār salām)
پس زول (Pas zool)
Arabian: سعد (Sa'ad)
Turkish: Topalak
English: Nutgrass
French: Souchet à tubercules

Similar species: *Cyperus esculentus* L.
Habitat: Growing on cultivated land, especially in irrigated crops, rice, up to 2000 m.
Tropics and subtropics of all continents.
Propagation: Perennial plant, reproduces by seeds and rhizome tubers, flowering from May to December.
Remarks: Different aspect on dry and flooded fields, one of the most important weeds in rice.
Hard to control: pre-emergence treatments with EPTC, dichlobenil, chlorthiamid, terbacil, bromacil; post-emergence treatments with 2,4-D, MSMA, glyphosate, amitrole in repeated applications.

Cyperaceae

Dipsacaceae

Cephalaria syriaca (L.) Schrad.   Dipsacaceae

Synonyms: *Cephalaria boissieri* Reuter, *Scabiosa syriaca* L.

Vernacular names:

Farsi: سرشکافته (Sarshekāfteh)

Arabian: طردان (Tardān)

Turkish: Pelemir, Zivan, Orun

English: Syrian scabious
Syrian cephalaria

French: Céphalarie

Similar species:

Habitat: Cornfields and waste places up to 1700 m. Mediterranean area, Iran.

Propagation: Annual, reproduces by seeds, flowering from April to May.

Remarks: Seeds poisonous, cause an unpleasant taste if mixed with flour.
Controlled by 2,4-D.

Dipsacaceae

Euphorbiaceae

Chrozophora tinctoria (L.) Raf. **Euphorbiaceae**

Synonyms: *Croton tinctoria* L., *Rhicinoides tinctoria* Moench. *Tournesolia tinctoria* Baill.

Vernacular names:

Farsi: کرش بو (Goosh-barreh)
Arabian: نيلي (Nilee)
Turkish: Boya otu, Bambul otu
English: Officinal croton
French: Croton des teinturiers

Similar species:

Habitat: Growing in orchards, vineyards and on waste places. Mediterranean area, Southwest Asia to India.

Propagation: Annual plant, reproduces by seeds, flowering from July to August.

Remarks: Leaves furnish a dye, whole plant poisonous. Controlled with pyrazon.

Euphorbiaceae

Euphorbiaceae

Euphorbia chamaesyce L.   Euphorbiaceae

Synonyms: *Euphorbia canescens* L

Vernacular names:

Farsi: شِبرَک (Shirak)
Arabian: لبن (Lubeen)
Turkish: Sütlüğen
English: Crenated spurge
French: Euphorbe

Similar species:

Habitat: Growing on cultivated land, especially lawns. Mediterranean plant. North Africa, Southwest Asia, Iran.

Propagation: Annual plant, reproduces by seeds, flowering from April to July.

Remarks: Controlled with 2,4-D.

Euphorbiaceae

Aegilops triuncialis L.

Gramineae

Synonyms: *Aegilops echinata* Presl., *Aegilops elongata* Lam., *Triticum triunciale* Gren. et Godr.

Vernacular names:

Farsi:
Arabian: شعير ابليس (Sha'eer Iblees)
Turkish: Sakalotu
English: Three-inch goats face grass
French: Egilops

Similar species: *Aegilops crassa* Boiss., *Aegilops ovata* L.

Habitat: Growing in and at the borders of cornfields. Circum-mediterranean plant. Areas with moderate climate in Southwest Asia.

Propagation: Annual plant reproduces by seeds. flowering April to June

Remarks:

Gramineae

Avena fatua L.   Gramineae

Synonyms: *Avena nigra* Wallr.

Vernacular names:

Farsi: يولاف (Yoolāf)
جودوسر (Jou do sar)

Arabian:

Turkish: Deli yulaf

English: Wild oat

French: Folle avoine

Similar species: *Avena sterilis* L., *Avena barbata* Pott

Habitat: Growing on moist, heavy soils in cornfields. East mediterranean plant. Europe, Asia, North Africa, North and South America.

Propagation: Annual plant, reproduces by seeds, flowering March to June.

Remarks: Provides a good forage on fallow. Controlled with triallate, benzoylpropethyl, chlorphenpropmethyl and barban.

Gramineae

Seed on page 103

Avena sterilis L.   Gramineae

Synonyms: *Avena syriaca* Boiss. et BL. MS

Vernacular names:

Farsi: يولاف (Yoolāf)

Arabian:

Turkish: Kısır yulaf

English: Great wild oat. Animated oats

French: Avoine stérile

Similar species: *Avena fatua* L., *Avena barbata* Pott

Habitat: Growing in fields, vineyards and waste places. Mediterranean plant. Mediterranean countries, Southwest Asia, England, Belgium, Netherlands, North Germany.

Propagation: Annual plant, reproduces by seeds, flowering March to June.

Remarks: Provides good forage on fallow. Species is very variable with two subspecies which are important in the mediterranean area: Avena sterilis L. ssp. ludoviciana (Dur.) Gill. et Magne and Avena sterilis L. ssp. macrocarpa (Moench) Briquet.

Gramineae

Seedling on page 101

A. fatua

A. sterilis ssp. ludoviciana

A. sterilis spp. macrocarpa

Gramineae

Brachiaria eruciformis (Sibth. et Sm.) Griseb.   Gramineae

Synonyms: *Brachiaria isachne* Stapf, *Echinochloa eruciforme* Reichb., *Panicum eruciforme* Sibth. et Sm., *Panicum isachne* Roth

Vernacular names:
Farsi: چیک واش (Chik-vāsh)
Arabian:
Turkish:
English: Signal grass
French:

Similar species:

Habitat: Growing on moist, fertile soils, in irrigated crops, orchards, vineyards, cottonfields and waste places.
Southwest Asia, Mediterranean countries.

Propagation: Annual plant, reproduces by seeds, flowering from June to October.

Remarks:

Gramineae

0.15 mm

Gramineae

Coix lacryma-jobi L.　　　　　　Gramineae

Synonyms:

Vernacular names:

Farsi: شال تسبیح (Shāl tasbih)

Arabian:

Turkish: Gözyaşı otu

English: Jobs tears

French: Larmilles

Similar species:

Habitat: Growing on moist places along irrigation ditches. South America, Southwest Asia, Iran.

Propagation: Annual plant, reproduces by seeds, flowering July to August.

Remarks: Seeds used for rosaries, sometimes cultivated.

Gramineae

Gramineae

Cynodon dactylon (L.) Pers. **Gramineae**

Synonyms: *Capriola dactylon* Kunze, *Panicum dactylon* L.

Vernacular names:
Farsi: مرغ (Margh)
Arabian: نجيل (Nejeel)
Turkish: Köpek dişi ayrığı
English: Bermuda grass
French: Chiendent dactyle, Chiendent à pied de poule

Similar species:

Habitat: Growing on fertile sandy soils in perennial crops, orchards, vineyards and lawns.
Cosmopolitan in subtropical and warm-moderate climates.

Propagation: Perennial plant, reproduces by seeds and aerial and underground runners, flowering throughout the year.

Remarks: Grown as forage crop and lawn grass. Juice used for medicinal purposes.
Hard to control because of its strong and numerous rhizomes.
Controlled with glyphosate, TCA, dalapon, uracils.

Gramineae

Gramineae

Digitaria sanguinalis Scop. Gramineae

Synonyms: *Dactylon sanguinale* Vill., *Panicum sanguinale* L., *Phalaris velutina* Forsk., *Syntherisma vulgare* Schrad.

Vernacular names:

Farsi: گاورس (Gāvers)

Arabian: ذنبة (Dafeerah)

Turkish: Çatal otu, Darı otu, Cavers otu

English: Crabgrass

French: Digitaire sanguinale

Similar species:

Habitat: Growing on moist, fertile, sandy soils in fields, gardens, lawns and irrigation ditches.
Circum mediterranean plant. Cosmopolite in temperate and warm zones.

Propagation: Annual plant, reproduces by seeds, flowering May to December.

Remarks: Controlled with alachlor, triazines, pebulate, TCA, IPC and trifluralin.

Gramineae

Echinochloa crus-galli (L.) Beauv.

Gramineae

Synonyms: *Hoplismenus crus-galli* Dum., *Panicum crus-corvi* L., *Panicum crus-galli* L.

Vernacular names:
Farsi: سوروف (Sooroof)
Arabian: دنيبه (Deneebah)
Turkish: Darıcan, Pirinç otu, Dineba
English: Barnyard grass
French: Pied de coq

Similar species: *Echinochloa colonum* (L.) Link

Habitat: Growing on moist rich, more or less sandy loam soils with good nitrogen supply in fields, orchards, gardens and paddy.
In moderate and warm climates cosmopolitan.

Propagation: Annual plant, reproduces by seeds, flowering May to November.

Remarks: One of the most important weeds in rice. Controlled with butylate, alachlor, triazines, pebulate, cycloate, TCA, IPC, molinate, butachlor, trifluralin, dichlobenil, propanil.

Gramineae

Eragrostis minor Host Gramineae

Synonyms: *Eragrostis poaeformis* Link, *Eragrostis poaeoides* Beauv., *Poa eragrostis* L.

Vernacular names:
Farsi:
Arabian:
Turkish: Ufak çayır güzeli
English: Spreading love grass
French: Eragrostis amourette

Similar species: *Eragrostis barrelieri* Dav., *Eragrostis cilianensis* (All.) Vign.-Lut.

Habitat: Growing on moist, fertile, sandy soils, irrigated fields. Mediterranean-submediterranean-continental plant, Mediterranean countries, South Russia, South Asia, North and Central America.

Propagation: Annual plant, reproduces by seeds, flowering August to September.

Remarks:

Gramineae

Lolium temulentum L.   Gramineae

Synonyms: *Bromus temulentus* Bernh., *Craepalia temulenta* Schrank, *Lolium annum* Gilib.

Vernacular names:

Farsi: عشرچن   ('Alafe chaman)
       چم   (Chacham)
       کیجدانه   (Gijdāneh)

Arabian: زُوان   (Zawān)

Turkish: Delice, Zivan

English: Darnel

French: Ivraie

Similar species: *Lolium multiflorum* Lam., *Lolium perenne* L.

Habitat: Growing on moist, fertile and calcarious loamy soils, Submediterranean-mediterranean plant.
Europe, North and South Africa, moderate areas in Asia, North and South America, Australia.

Propagation: Annual plant, reproduces by seeds, flowering from April to July.

Remarks: Seeds poisonous.
Since seeds survive in soil for only one year, best control is by proper purification of seed. Chemical control with chlortoluron.

Gramineae

Gramineae 118

Phalaris brachystachys Link   Gramineae

Synonyms: *Phalaris quadrivalvis* Lag

Vernacular names:

Farsi: بذرک کاناری (Bazrak Kānārā'ee)

Arabian:

Turkish:

English: Short-spiked canary grass

French: Alpiste

Similar species: *Phalaris minor* Retz., *Phalaris paradoxa* L.

Habitat: Growing in cornfields.
Mediterranean countries, Southwest Asia.

Propagation: Annual plant, reproduces by seeds, flowering March to June.

Remarks: Controlled with nitrofen, pebulate, cycloate.

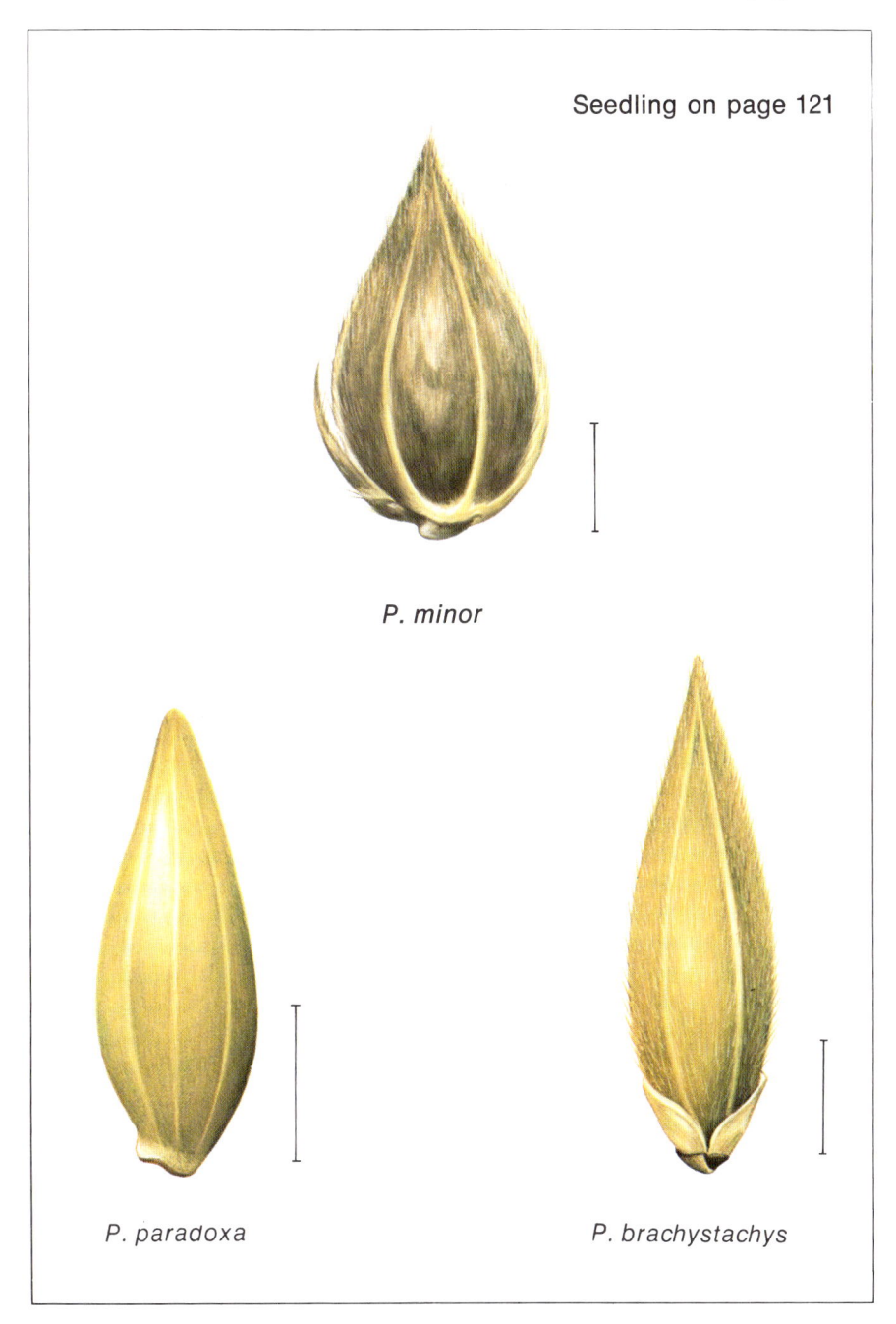

Gramineae

Seedling on page 121

P. minor

P. paradoxa

P. brachystachys

Gramineae

Phalaris minor Retz.   Gramineae

Synonyms:

Vernacular names:

Farsi: ﻼرﯾس (Falāris)
ﺑذرک (Bazrak)

Arabian:

Turkish: Küçük daneli kuş yemi

English: Lesser canary grass

French: Petit Phalaris

Similar species: *Phalaris brachystachys* Link, *Phalaris paradoxa* L.

Habitat: Growing on sandy alluvial soils in cornfields.
Tolerates saline soils.
Mediterranean countries, Southwest Asia.

Propagation: Annual plant, reproduces by seeds, flowering March to June.

Remarks: Controlled with nitrofen, pebulate, cycloate.

Gramineae

Seeds on page 119

Setaria glauca (L.) Beauv.   Gramineae

Synonyms: *Chaetochloa glauca* Nash, *Panicum glaucum* L., *Pennisetum glaucum* R. Br., Setaria *lutescens* (Weigel) F. T. Hubb., *Setaria pallidifusca* Stapf.

Vernacular names:

Farsi: اسب واش (Asb vāsh)

Arabian: شعرالنار (Sh'ar al Fār)

Turkish: Sıçan saçı, Sarı tüylü darı

English: Yellow foxtail, yellow bristlegrass

French: Setaire glauque

Similar species: *Setaria verticillata* (L.) Beauv., *Setaria viridis* (L.) Beauv.

Habitat: Growing on rich, sandy soils in cultivated land. Submediterranean-mediterranean plant. In warm zones nearly cosmopolitan.

Propagation: Annual plant, reproduces by seeds, flowering May to September.

Remarks: Controlled with butylate, alachlor, pebulate, triazines, TCA, IPC and trifluralin.

Gramineae

Setaria verticillata (L.) Beauv.   **Gramineae**

Synonyms: *Chaetochloa verticillata* Nash, *Panicum verticillatum* L., *Setaria panicea* Schinz et Thellg.

Vernacular names:

Farsi:

Arabian: فج النار (Qameh al Fār)

Turkish: Kirpi darı, Arnavut darısı

English: Bristly foxtail

French: Setaire verticillée

Similar species: *Setaria glauca* (L.) Beauv., *Setaria viridis* (L.) Beauv.

Habitat: Growing on fertile, mostly sandy loam soils in gardens, cultivated fields and waste places.
In warm zones nearly cosmopolitan.

Propagation: Annual plant, reproduces by seeds, flowering May to September.

Remarks: Controlled with triazines, pebulate, TCA, IPC and trifluralin.

Gramineae

Gramineae

Setaria viridis (L.) Beauv. — Gramineae

Synonyms: *Chaetochloa viridis* Nash, *Panicum viride* L.

Vernacular names:

Farsi: ارزن وحشی (Arzan vahshee)

Arabian: دبل النار (Del al Fār)

Turkish: Yeşil cin darı, Yeşil tüylü darı

English: Green foxtail, Green Bristlegrass

French: Setaire verte

Similar species: *Setaria glauca* (L.) Beauv., *Setaria verticillata* (L.) Beauv.

Habitat: Growing on rich, sandy soils in gardens, orchards, tea, cornfields and along ditches.
Eurasian-mediterranean plant. Europe, Sibiria, East and North Africa and nearly all zones with moderate climate.

Propagation: Annual plant, reproduces by seeds, flowering May to September.

Remarks: Controlled with butylate, alachlor, triazines, pebulate, TCA, IPC and trifluralin.

Gramineae

Gramineae

Sorghum halepense (L.) Pers.   Gramineae

Synonyms: *Andropogon arundinaceum* Scop., *Andropogon avenaceus* Humb. et Kunth, *Andropogon halepensis* Brot., *Holcus exiguus* Forsk., *Holcus halepensis* L., *Trachypogon avenaceus* Nees

Vernacular names:

Farsi: تیان (Qiāq)
حلیل (Halit)

Arabian: حشيشة الفرس (Hashishet el Faras)

Turkish: Kanyaş

English: Johnson grass

French: Sorgho d'Alep

Similar species: —

Habitat: Growing on cultivated land with perennial crops e. g. vineyards and orchards, also along ditches and on fallow.
Circum-mediterranean plant. South and Southeast Europe, North and East Africa, Southwest to Southeast Asia, China, North and Central America.

Propagation: Perennial plant, reproduces by seeds and rhizomes, flowering from May to October.

Remarks: In some areas grown as forage crop. Under certain conditions, for example water stress or mild frost, plant is poisonous to stock. Plant is hard to kill because of its enormous rhizome masses. Controlled with simazine + atrazine and trifluralin in high doses, glyphosate.

Gramineae

Alhagi camelorum Fisch

Leguminosae

Synonyms: *Alhagi persarum* Boiss. et Buhse. *Alhagi pseudalhagi* (Bieb.) Desv., *Hedysarum pseudalhagi* Bieb.

Vernacular names:

Farsi: خارشتر (Khār shotor)

Arabian: عَقول ('Aquol)

Turkish: Deve dikeni

English: Camelthorn

French: Chameau-sainfoin

Similar species:

Habitat: Growing on fallow, edges of ditches, waste places, tolerating saline soils, up to 1200 m.
Irano-Turanian plant, West Caucasia, West Sibiria, Iran, Central and East Asia.

Propagation: Perennial plant, reproduces by seeds, flowering from May to September.

Remarks: Used as fuel, grazed by sheep and camels, excreted juice used for medicinal purposes.
Controlled by pre-emergence treatments with atrazine and post-emergence treatment with 2,4-D.

Leguminosae

Leguminosae 132

Coronilla scorpioides (L.) Koch **Leguminosae**

Synonyms: *Ornithopus scorpioides* L.

Vernacular names:

Farsi:
Arabian:
Turkish:
English: Coronilla
French: Queue de Scorpion

Similar species:

Habitat: Growing on cultivated and disturbed ground, in fields, gardens and waste places up to 1000 m.
Circum-mediterranean plant, Central and South Europe, Caucasia, North Africa, West Syria, South Iran.

Propagation: Annual plant, reproduces by seeds, flowering March to July.

Remarks: Controlled with 2,4-D.

Leguminosae

Leguminosae

Glycyrrhiza glabra L.   Leguminosae

Synonyms: *Liquiritia officinalis* Moench

Vernacular names:

Farsi: مَتکی (Matkee)
شیرین بیان (Shirin Bayān)

Arabian:

Turkish: Meyan kökü, Meyan otu

English: Common liquorice

French: Réglisse glabre

Similar species: *Glycyrrhiza glandulifera* Waldst. et Kit.

Habitat: Growing on alluvial soils and sand dunes, in cornfields and fallow up to 1800 m.
South Europe, South Russia, North Africa, Southwest, Central and East Asia.

Propagation: Perennial plant, reproduces by seeds and underground runners, flowering May to June.

Remarks: In some regions grown for medicinal purposes. Beverages are made of root extracts. Poisonous to lifestock.

Leguminosae

Leguminosae

Goebelia alopecuroides L. Leguminosae

Synonyms:

Vernacular names:

Farsi: تلخ بیان (Tālkh bayān)

Arabian:

Turkish:

English:

French:

Similar species: *Glycyrrhiza glabra* L.

Habitat: Edges of cornfields, fallow, waste land.
Greece, South Russia, Southwest and East Asia.

Propagation: Perennial, reproduces by seeds and roots, flowering in May.

Remarks: Grazed by stock.
Controlled by repeated applications of 2,4-D.

Leguminosae

Lathyrus aphaca L.   Leguminosae

Synonyms: *Aphaca marmorata* Alef., *Aphaca vulgaris* Alef., *Aphaca vulgaris* Presl., *Lathyrus dispermus* Boiss., *Lathyrus polyanthus* Boiss. et Bl., *Lathyrus segetum* Lam., *Orobus aphaca* Döll.

Vernacular names:
Farsi: خَلَر (Khollar)
Arabian: صام البرج (Hamām el Burj)
Turkish: Mürdümük, Tavşan bezelyesi
English: Yellow vetchling
French: Gesse aphaca

Similar species:

Habitat: Growing on fertile, calcarious loam soils, on meadows and cornfields, from sea level to 1800 m.
West, Central and South Europe, Southwest and Central Asia, North Africa.

Propagation: Annual plant, reproduces by seeds, flowering from May to June.

Remarks: In some areas grown as forage crop. Seeds poisonous. Controlled by 2,4-D.

Leguminosae

Leguminosae

Lathyrus blepharicarpus Boiss.   Leguminosae

Synonyms: *Lathyrus amphicarpos* L.

Vernacular names:

Farsi:

Arabian:

Turkish:

English: Wing-podded vetchling

French: Gesse

Similar species: *Lathyrus cicera* L., *Lathyrus marmoratus* Boiss. et Bl.

Habitat: Growing in fields and on grassy places. East mediterranean plant. Turkey to Tunisia.

Propagation: Annual plant, reproduces by seeds, flowering from April to May.

Remarks: Seeds eaten by man. Controlled with 2,4-D.

Leguminosae

Leguminosae

Lathyrus ochrus DC.   Leguminosae

Synonyms: *Clymenum ochrus* Alef., *Lathyrus currentifolius* Lam., *Ochrus pallida* Pers., *Ochrus uniflorus* Moench, *Pisum ochrus* L.

Vernacular names:

Farsi: خلر   (Khollar)

Arabian:

Turkish:

English: Yellow pea

French: Ocre, Gesse ochre

Similar species:

Habitat: Growing in cornfields, dry and grassy places and roadsides from sea level up to 50 m.
Circum-mediterranean plant. Mediterranean countries.

Propagation: Annual plant, reproduces by seeds, flowering in April.

Remarks: Sometimes cultivated as forage crop.
Controlled with 2,4-D.

Leguminosae

Leguminosae 144

Medicago hispida Gaertn.　　　　　　　　　**Leguminosae**

Synonyms: *Medicago denticulata* Willd., *Medicago polymorpha* Willd.

Vernacular names:
Farsi: بومجه وحی (Yunje koohi)
Arabian: نَفَل (Nafal)
Turkish: Kaba yonca
English: Bur clover
French: Luzerne hispide

Similar species:

Habitat: Cultivated and fallow fields, waste places up to 900 m. Mediterranean area, Southwest and Central Asia, Atlantic coast from Portugal to England, Netherlands and Belgium, Chile, Argentina.

Propagation: Annual plant, reproduces by seeds, flowering March to June.

Remarks: Plant is a most variable species. In some regions grown as forage crop.
Controlled with atrazine, pyrazon and 2,4-D.

Leguminosae

Melilotus albus Med. Leguminosae

Synonyms: *Melilotus leucantha* Koch, *Melilotus melanosperma* Besser, *Melilotus rugosus* Gilib., *Melilotus rugulosa* Willd., *Melilotus vulgaris* Willd.

Vernacular names:

Farsi: يونجه زرد (Yoonje zard)

Arabian: حندقوق (Handaqooq)

Turkish: Aktaş yoncası

English: White melilot, Sweet melilot

French: Mélilot blanc

Similar species:

Habitat: Growing on fertile loamy soils with good nitrogen supply, especially in irrigated crops, orchards and waste places. Eurasian-continental-submediterranean plant, Europe, West Asia to West Sibiria, Tibet, India, Egypt.

Propagation: Biennial plant, reproduces by seeds, flowering from May to September.

Remarks: Cultivated in Lebanon for pipe-stems because of the fragrant odour of its woods.
Controlled with 2,4-D and pyrazon.

Leguminosae

Leguminosae

Prosopis stephaniana (Willd.) Kunth — Leguminosae

Synonyms: *Acacia stephaniana* Willd., *Lagonychium stephanianum* Bieb., *Mimosa farcta* Banks et Sol., *Lagonychium farctum* (Banks et Sol.) Bobr., *Prosopis farcta* (Banks et Sol.) Macbride

Vernacular names:
Farsi: جغجغه (Jeghjegheh)   كويره (Kevireh)
Arabian: شلشلوي (Shilshillawi)
Turkish: Burgulu fasulye, Çeti
English:
French:

Similar species:

Habitat: Typical plant of the substeppe flora of the Irano-Turanian zone. Growing on fertile Sierozem soils in cultivated areas of low altitude, especially in wheat, along roads and ditches and on fallow. Southwest and Central Asia. Egypt, Cyprus.

Propagation: Perennial plant, reproduces by seeds, flowering from May to August.

Remarks: Grazed by stock, and used as fuel.
Hard to kill because of its deep reaching roots. Controlled by 2,4-D in repeated applications.

Leguminosae

Leguminosae

Scorpiurus sulcata L. Leguminosae

Synonyms: *Scorpiurus minima* A. Los, *Scorpiurus muricatus* L. var. *subvillosus* (L.) Fiori, *Scorpiurus subvillosa* L.

Vernacular names:
Farsi:
Arabian: ألعقربان (Alaqrabān)
Turkish:
English: Furrowed caterpillar
French: Scorpiure, Chenillette

Similar species: *Scorpiurus vermiculatus* L.

Habitat: Grows on loamy soils on cultivated land and fallow fields up to 800 m.
Mediterranean countries, Transcaucasia, Syrian desert, North Iraq, South Iran, East Africa.

Propagation: Annual plant, reproduces by seeds, flowering from April to May.

Remarks: Plant is an extremely variable species.
Controlled with 2,4-D, partly controlled with pyrazon, atrazine.

Leguminosae

S. vermiculatus L.

Leguminosae

Vicia lutea L.   Leguminosae

Synonyms: *Hypechusa lutea* Alef., *Wiggersia lutea* Gaertn.

Vernacular names:

Farsi:

Arabian: بخرا   (Bakhrā)

Turkish:

English: Yellow vetch, Rough-podded vetch

French: Vesce jaune

Similar species:

Habitat: Growing on calcarious loamy soils in cornfields. Mediterranean plant. Mediterranean countries, West and Central Europe.

Propagation: Annual plant, reproduces by seeds and runners, flowering in May.

Remarks: Controlled with 2,4-D.

Leguminosae

Leguminosae 154

Vicia sativa L. Leguminosae

Synonyms: *Vicia communis* Rouy

Vernacular names:

Farsi: كاشت (Māshak)

Arabian: بسيلة (Bselah)

Turkish:

English: Common vetch

French: Vesce commune

Similar species: *Vicia angustifolia* Grufb.

Habitat: Growing in fields and waste places.
East mediterranean plant. Europe, West Asia, North and South Africa, Australia, New Zealand, North and South America.

Propagation: Annual to perennial plant, reproduces by seeds and runners, flowering March to April.

Remarks: Grown as forage crop. As weed an escape from cultivation. Species is very variable.
Controlled with 2,4-D and pyrazon.

Leguminosae

Vicia villosa Roth

Leguminosae

Synonyms: *Vicia varia* Host

Vernacular names:
Farsi: باشک گل خوشه‌ای (Māshake gol khooshe'ee)
Arabian:
Turkish:
English: Winter vetch
French: Vesce velue

Similar species: *Vicia cracca* L.

Habitat: Growing on moist sand and loam soils, cornfields, banks, irrigated crops up to 1700 m.
South and Central Europe, North Africa, Central and South Russia, Southwest Asia, Iran.

Propagation: Annual or biennial plant, reproduces by seeds, flowering June to November.

Remarks: The plant is very variable with several subspecies. Sometimes cultivated as forage crop.
Controlled with 2,4-D, pyrazon.

Leguminosae

Lythraceae

Ammannia baccifera L.   Lythraceae

Synonyms: *Ammannia aegyptiaca* Willd.

Vernacular names:

Farsi: کورچین ایاغی   (Goorchin ayāghi)

Arabian: رجل حمامة   (Rejel Hamāmeh)

Turkish: Güvercin ayağı

English: Tooth cup

French: Ammannie

Similar species: *Ammannia senegalensis* Lam.

Habitat: Growing near warm sulphur springs, streamsides, in rice fields and wet places.
North Iraq, South Russia, North Iran, Central and East Asia.

Propagation: Annual plant, reproduces by seeds, flowering August to March.

Remarks: Leaves cause blisters on skin.

Lythraceae

Malvaceae

Abutilon avicennae Gaertn. — Malvaceae

Synonyms: *Abutilon teophrastii* Med., *Sida abutilon* L., *Sida tiliifolia* Fischer

Vernacular names:

Farsi: دیوکنف (Div kenaf)

Arabian: عوس الغنم ('Aos el Ghanam)

Turkish: Hind keneviri

English: American velvet leaf

French: Abutilon ordinaire,
Guimauve jaune

Similar species:

Habitat: On irrigated land, along irrigated ditches.
South East Europe to Central Asia, Africa, Australia, North America.

Propagation: Annual plant, reproduces by seeds, flowering from June to October.

Remarks: Once grown as fiber crop and for medicinal use in China Controlled by phenoxy compounds.

Malvaceae

Malvaceae

162

Hibiscus trionum L. **Malvaceae**

Synonyms: *Ketmia trionum* Scop., *Trionum diffusum* Moench

Vernacular names:
Farsi:
Arabian: تيل شيطاني (Teel sheytāni)
Turkish: Şeytan keneviri
English: Flower of an hour, Bladder hibiscus
French: Ketmie d'Afrique

Similar species:

Habitat: On cultivated land up to 1000 m, especially in irrigated fields and gardens.
Balkan, Bulgaria, Romania, Cyprus, South Russia, Southwest and Central Asia, Australia, Africa, North America.

Propagation: Annual plant, reproduces by seeds, flowering from June to September.

Remarks: Easy to control with 2,4-D and contact herbicides, pre-emergence treatment with simazine, diuron, pebulate and pyrazon.

Malvaceae

Malva neglecta Wallr. Malvaceae

Synonyms: *Malva rotundifolia* L., *Malva vulgaris* Fries

Vernacular names:
Farsi: بنیرک (Panirak)
Arabian: خبیزه بری (Khobeyzah Barre)
Turkish: Cüce yabani ebe gömeci, Kıssa ebegümeci
English: Dwarf mallow
French: Mauve des chemins

Similar species: *Malva parviflora* L.

Habitat: Growing on moist, fertile loamy soils with good nitrogen supply, fields, gardens, steppe, roadsides, waste places up to 2000 m.
Eurasian-suboceanien plant. Europe, Northwest Africa, Southwest Asia.

Propagation: Annual to perennial plant, reproduces by seeds, flowering March to May.

Remarks: Flowers used for medicinal purposes.

Malvaceae

Orobanchaceae

Orobanche aegyptiaca Pers. **Orobanchaceae**

Synonyms: *Orobanche longiflora* Pers., *Phelipaea aegyptiaca* Walp.

Vernacular names:

Farsi: كل جاليز (Gole jāleez)

Arabian: هَالوك (Hālouk)

Turkish:

English: Egyptian broomrape

French:

Similar species: *Orobanche ramosa* L.

Habitat: Root parasite on tobacco, tomatoes, melons, peas and other Solanaceae, Cucurbitaceae and Leguminosae. Southwest Asia, Iran to India.

Propagation: Annual to perennial plant, reproduces by seeds, flowering February to September.

Remarks:

Orobanchaceae

Early stage of development on root of tomato

0.25 mm

Orobanchaceae

Orobanche cernua Loefl. **Orobanchaceae**

Synonyms: *Orobanche cumana* Wallr., *Orobanche hispanica* Boiss.

Vernacular names:

Farsi: كل جاليز (Gole jāleez)

Arabian: هالوك (Hālouk)

Turkish:

English: Drooping broomrape

French:

Similar species:

Habitat: Root parasite growing on tobacco and sunflower, also on other Solanaceae and Compositae.
Mediterranean countries, Asia from Russia to India, Australia.

Propagation: Annual plant, reproduces by seeds, flowering May to September.

Remarks: Resistant cultivars of sunflower known.

Orobanchaceae

Early stage of development on root of tobacco

0.25 mm

Orobanchaceae

Orobanche crenata Forsk.　　　　　　　　Orobanchaceae

Synonyms: *Orobanche klugei* Schmitz et Regel, *Orobanche pelargonii* Caldesi, *Orobanche picta* Wilms, *Orobanche pruinosa* Lapeyr., *Orobanche segetum* Spruner, *Orobanche speciosa* DC et Lam.

Vernacular names:

Farsi: كل جاليز　　(Gole jāleez)

Arabian: هَالوك　　(Hālouk)

Turkish: Beyaz çiçekli canavar otu

English: Scalloped broomrape

French: Orobanche blanc
Belle Orobanche

Similar species:

Habitat: Root parasite growing on broadbeans and other Leguminosae and on carrots.
Circum-mediterranean plant. Mediterranean countries, Iraq, Iran.

Propagation: Annual to perennial plant, reproduces by seeds, flowering February to June.

Remarks:

Orobanchaceae

Early stage of development on root of Broad bean

Orobanche ramosa L. Orobanchaceae

Synonyms: *Kopsia ramosa* (L.) Dum., *Lathraea phelipaea* Forsk., *Orobanche brassicae* Novopokr., *Orobanche mutelii* F. W. Schultz, *Phelipaea mutelii* Reuter, *Phelipaea ramosa* (L.) C. A. Mey.

Vernacular names:
Farsi: سل جالیز (Gole jāleez)
Arabian: هالوك (Hālouk)
Turkish: Mavi çiçekli canavar otu
English: Branched broomrape
French: Orobanche du chanvre

Similar species: *Orobanche aegyptiaca* Pers.

Habitat: Root parasite growing on carrots, sunflower, tobacco, tomatoes and many non crop plants, especially in humus sandy loam soils with high nitrogen level.

Circum-mediterranean plant. Mediterranean countries, North America, Central Europe, New Zealand.

Propagation: Annual to perennial plant, reproduces by seeds, flowering May to September.

Remarks:

Orobanchaceae

Early stage of development on root of tomato

0,25 mm

Papaveraceae

Fumaria officinalis L.   **Papaveraceae**

Synonyms:

Vernacular names:

Farsi: شاتَرِ (Shātareh)

Arabian: كَسفارةُ الحَمّار (Kasfāret al Hammār)

Turkish: Şahtere

English: Common fumitory

French: Fumeterre

Similar species: Many other *Fumaria* spp.

Habitat: Growing on moist, fertile loam soils, in fields and vineyards up to 700 m.
Eurasian-suboceanien plant. Europe, Transcaucasia, Iran, North Africa, North America.

Propagation: Annual plant, reproduces by seeds, flowering March to May.

Remarks: Leaves used for medicinal purposes.
Controlled with DNOC.

Papaveraceae

Phytolacca americana L. **Phytolaccaceae**

Synonyms: *Phytolacca decandra* L.

Vernacular names:
Farsi:
Arabian: عنب أمريكي (Enab Amriki)
Turkish: Şeceri boyası otu
English: Virginian poke, Pigeon-berry
French: Raisin d'Amerique

Similar species:

Habitat: Growing on fields, rich pastures, open places in woodlands, along ditches and roads up to 500 m.
North America, Mexico, South and Central Europe, Transcaucasia, Iran, Cyprus, North Africa.

Propagation: Perennial plant, reproduces by seeds, flowering from July to September.

Remarks: Cultivated as ornamental and for a dye obtained from the berries. Whole plant poisonous, used for medicinal purposes. Relatively resistant to hormones, controlled with amitrole.

Phytolaccaceae

Plantago lanceolata L.   Plantaginaceae

Synonyms: *Arnoglossum lanceolatum* (L.) S. F. Gray. *Plantago flexuosa* Gaud., *Plantago lanceaefolia* Salisb.. *Plantago longistipes* Royle, *Plantago sylvatica* Martius

Vernacular names:
Farsi: بارهنگ (Bārhang)
      کاردی (Kardı)
Arabian: إدهام الكبش (Idham el Kabbsh)
Turkish: Dar yapraklı sinir otu
English: Ribgrass, Narrow-leaved plantain
French: Plantain, Oreille de lièvre

Similar species: Numerous *Plantago*-species

Habitat: Growing on moist, fertile loam and sandy soils, orchards, irrigation ditches, cultivated fields, roadsides. Temperate zones of the world.

Propagation: Perennial plant, reproduces by seeds, flowering from March to July.

Remarks: Seeds, fresh and dry leaves used for medicinal purposes. Controlled with 2,4-D.

Plantaginaceae

Polygonaceae

Emex spinosus (L.) Campd. **Polygonaceae**

Synonyms: *Rumex glaber* Forsk., *Rumex spinosus* L.

Vernacular names:

Farsi: ترب کوهی (Torob koohee)
هویج صحرائی (Havij sahrā'ee)

Arabian: طرس العجوز (Derrs al'Agouz)

Turkish:

English: Prickly dock

French: Emex épineux

Similar species:

Habitat: Growing on sandy places near sea level in fields, citrus groves and gardens.
Mediterranean countries.

Propagation: Annual plant, reproduces by seeds, flowering from October to June.

Remarks: Troublesome to grazing stock.
Controlled with 2,4-D and MCPA in the rosette stage, in later stages relatively resistant.

Polygonaceae

Portulaca oleracea L.   Portulacaceae

Synonyms:

Vernacular names:

Farsi: خرفه   (Khorfeh)

Arabian: رِجلة   (Rijleh)

Turkish: Semiz otu

English: Common purslane

French: Pourpier potager

Similar species:

Habitat: Growing on fertile, sandy soils, cultivated ground and waste places up to 1700 m.
Cosmopolitan plant.

Propagation: Annual plant, reproduces by seeds, flowering from May to October.

Remarks: Often collected and also grown as a vegetable. Controlled with 2,4-D, pebulate, pyrazone, glyphosate and trifluralin.

Portulacaceae

Primulaceae

Anagallis arvensis L. Primulaceae

Synonyms:

Vernacular names:
Farsi: بذرک وحشی (Bazrak vahshee)
Arabian: عين الجمل ('Ayen al Jamel)
Turkish: Tarla farekulağı
English: Pimpernel
French: Mouron des champs

Similar species: *Anagallis monelli* L.

Habitat: Growing on rich moist, humus sand or loam soils in fields and gardens.

Circum-mediterranean plant, Europe, moderate West and Central Asia, North and South Africa, North and Central America, South Brasilia, West Australia, Tasmania.

Propagation: Annual plant, reproduces by seeds and aerial runners, flowering February to June.

Remarks: Controlled with 2,4-D.

Primulaceae

Ranunculus arvensis L.

Ranunculaceae

Synonyms:

Vernacular names:

Farsi:

Arabian: زغلانتة (Zaghalānta)

Turkish: Düğün

English: Corn crowfoot

French: Renoncule des champs

Similar species: *Ranunculus repens* L.

Habitat: Growing in segetal habitats, on calcarious loam soils, often in cornfields up to 1850 m.
Mediterranean-irano-turanian plant. Europe, Southwest Asia. North Africa, Turkestan.

Propagation: Annual plant, reproduces by seeds, flowering March to April.

Remarks: Controlled with MCPA.

Ranunculaceae

Rosaceae

Hultemia persica (Gmel.) Bornm.   **Rosaceae**

Synonyms: *Hultemia berberifolia* Pall., *Rosa persica* J. F. Gmel., *Rosa simplicifolia* Salisb.

Vernacular names:
Farsi: درک (Varak)
Arabian:
Turkish:
English:
French:

Similar species:

Habitat: Growing on cultivated land, especially cornfields, on fertile loamy soils, waste places on formerly cultivated land.

Propagation: Perennial plant, reproduces by seeds, flowering from May to July.

Remarks: Possibly controlled by repeated treatments with 2,4-D.

Rosaceae

Rubiaceae

Galium tricorne Stokes — Rubiaceae

Synonyms: *Galium tricornutum* Dandy, *Valantia triflora* Lam.

Vernacular names:

Farsi: بی‌ترخ (Bitirākh)
Arabian: ذبيك (Dobbeyk)
Turkish: Köşeli yapraklı, Yoğurt otu
English: Rough bedstraw
French: Gaillet à trois corne

Similar species: *Galium aparine* L., *Galium saccharatum* All.

Habitat: Growing on fertile and mostly calcarious loamy soils, Submediterranean-mediterranean plant.
South and Central Europe, Southwest Asia, North Africa.

Propagation: Annual plant, reproduces by seeds, flowering from May to October.

Remarks: Controlled with CMPP.

Rubiaceae

Rubiaceae

Rubia tinctorum L.   **Rubiaceae**

Synonyms:

Vernacular names:

Farsi:
Arabian: فوه (Fowwah)
Turkish: Kızıl boya, Kök boyası, Fuvve
English: Dyer's madder
French: Garance-sauvage

Similar species: *Rubia peregrina* L.

Habitat: Growing on moist and fertile soils, along ditches. Mediterranean countries.

Propagation: Perennial plant, reproduces by seeds and roots, flowering May to July.

Remarks: Formerly grown for the dye obtained from the roots.

Rubiaceae

Scrophulariaceae 194

Linaria triphylla (L.) Mill. **Scrophulariaceae**

Synonyms: *Antirrhinum triphyllum* L.

Vernacular names:

Farsi:
Arabian:
Turkish:
English: Three-leaved toadflax
French: Linaire

Similar species:

Habitat: Growing in cornfields and vineyards. Mediterranean plant, South Europe, Israel, Morocco to Libya.

Propagation: Annual plant, reproduces by seeds, flowering from February to June.

Remarks:

Scrophulariaceae

Solanaceae

Datura stramonium L.　　　　　　　　　　**Solanaceae**

Synonyms: *Stramonium spinosum* Lam.

Vernacular names:
Farsi: تاتوره (Tatooreh)
Arabian: داتورة (Datooreh)
Turkish: Şeytan elması
English: Jimson weed, Thorn apple
French: Pomme épineuse

Similar species: *Datura metel* L.

Habitat: Growing on fertile clay, loam and sandy soils with high nitrogen levels, on cultivated land, especially in irrigated fields, roadsides, waste places.
Central and Southern Europe, Africa, Asia, North America, New Zealand, moderate and warm regions of all continents.

Propagation: Annual, reproduces from seeds, flowering from May to October.

Remarks: All parts of plant, especially the seeds, poisonous. Grown for medical uses.
Controlled by simazine, dinoseb, 2,4-DB, MCPA + 2,3,6-TBA, pyrazon.

Solanaceae

Solanaceae

Solanum nigrum L. **Solanaceae**

Synonyms: *Solanum judaicum* Bess., *Solanum alatum* Moench

Vernacular names:

Farsi: تاجريزي   انگورک   (Tāj-rizi) (Angoorak)
Arabian: عنب الديب   (Inabb el Deeb)
Turkish: Köpek üzümü, İt üzümü, Köpek memesi
English: Black nightshade
French: Morelle noire

Similar species:

Habitat: Growing on moist, fertile sand and clay soils with good nitrogen supply, irrigated crops.
Cosmopolitan.

Propagation: Annual plant, reproduces by seeds, flowering throughout the year.

Remarks: Leaves and green berries toxic.
Controlled with 2,4-D, pyrazon, phenmedipham and urea compounds.

Solanaceae

Ammi maius L. — Umbelliferae

Synonyms: *Aethusa ammi* Sprengel, *Ammi baeberi* Hoeq., *Ammi boeberi* Hoekert, *Ammi broussonetii* DC, *Ammi cicutifolium* Willd., *Ammi elatum* Salisb., *Apium ammi* Crantz, *Apium ammi maius* Crantz, *Selinum ammoides* E. H. L. Krause, *Sison maior* Eaton et Wright, *Visnaga vulgaris* Bubani

Vernacular names:

Farsi: وایه (Vāyeh)

Arabian: خله شيطانيه (Khaleh Sheytanyah)

Turkish: Karaman kimyonu

English: Common bishop's weed

French: Grand Ajoua

Similar species: *Ammi visnaga* (l.) Lam.

Habitat: Growing in cornfields, vineyards, along ditches and on waste places up to 700 m.
Mediterranean plant. South Europe, North Africa, Ethiopia, West Syria, Iraq, Iran, America, New Zealand, Australia.

Propagation: Annual plant, reproduces by seeds, flowering from April to July.

Remarks: Suspected to be harmful to cattle when eaten in quantity.

Umbelliferae

Umbelliferae

Astoma seselifolium DC.   **Umbelliferae**

Synonyms:

Vernacular names:

Farsi:

Arabian: سمرة   (Sammrah)

Turkish:

English: Astoma

French:

Similar species: *Scaligera cretica* Boiss.

Habitat: Growing in cornfields. North Africa.

Propagation: Perennial plant, reproduces by seeds, flowering April to May.

Remarks: Root globular.

Umbelliferae

Umbelliferae

Lisaea syriaca Boiss. **Umbelliferae**

Synonyms: *Caucalis strigosa* Russ., *Lisaea heterocarpa* var. *syriaca* Post, *Lisaea strigosa* (Banks et Sol.) Eig.

Vernacular names:

Farsi:

Arabian:

Turkish:

English: Great bur parsley

French:

Similar species:

Habitat: Growing in cornfields, steppe and waste places up to 1750 m.
Syrian desert, Palestine, North Iraq, North Iran, typical Irano-turanian plant.

Propagation: Annual plant, reproduces by seeds, flowering in May.

Remarks:

Umbelliferae

Umbelliferae

Scandix pecten-veneris L.   Umbelliferae

Synonyms: *Chaerophyllum pecten-veneris* Crantz, *Chaerophyllum rostratum* Lam., *Myrrhis pecten-veneris* All., *Pecten veneris* Lam., *Pectinaria vulgaris* Bernh., *Scandix cornuta* Gilib., *Scandix pecten* Scop., *Scandix pectinifera* Stokes, *Scandix pectiniformis* St. Lager, *Scandix rostrata* Salisb., *Scandix vulgaris* S. F. Gray, *Selinum pecten* E. H. L. Krause, *Wylia pecten-veneris* Bubani

Vernacular names:

Farsi:

Arabian: مشط الراعي   (Musht el Ra'ey)

Turkish: Zühre tarağı, Çoban tarağı

English: Shepherds needle

French: Peigne de Vénus

Similar species: *Scandix iberica* Bieb.
Habitat: Growing on rich calcarious soils in cornfields, tree nurseries and along roads up to 1000 m.
Mediteranean-submediterranean plant. West, Central and South Europe, North Africa, from Southwest Asia eastwards to the Himalaya, South Africa, New Zealand.
Propagation: Annual plant, reproduces by seeds, flowering February to May.
Remarks: The needle-like seeds are reported to have caused sores in the mouths of animals.
Controlled by 2,4-D.

Umbelliferae

Zygophyllaceae

Peganum harmala L.   **Zygophyllaceae**

Synonyms:

Vernacular names:

Farsi: اسـفند (Esfand)
Arabian: قرمل (Harmal)
Turkish: Üzerlik otu, Mahmur
English: African rue
French: Rue Sauvage

Similar species:

Habitat: Growing abundantly in the outskirts of villages in the steppe, on sandy, sometimes saline places up to 1500 m.
South Europe, North Africa, Southwest Asia, eastwards to Tibet, North America.

Propagation: Perennial plant, reproduces by seeds, flowering in spring and autumn.

Remarks: Poisonous to stock. Leaves used for medicinal purposes, seeds used as incense.

Zygophyllaceae

Tribulus terrestris L.

Zygophyllaceae

Synonyms:

Vernacular names:

Farsi: خارخسک (Khār Khasak)

Arabian: دقن الشيخ (Dagn esh-Sheikh)
خرطوم النعجة (Kharshoom en-Na'ja)

Turkish: Demir dikeni

English: Puncture vine

French: Croix de Malte

Similar species: *Tribulus longipetalus* Viv., *Tribulus mollis* Ehrenb.

Habitat: Dry areas of most parts of the tropics, subtropics and warmer temperate regions of all continents. On cultivated land; mainly on fallow, waste places, along roads and on poor grassland. Mediterranean countries, Southwest Asia, USA.

Propagation: Annual plant, reproduces by seeds, flowering from April to September.

Remarks: Very deep reaching tap root, leaves poisonous to sheep, spiny fruits troublesome to feet of man and animals, even punctured tires reported. Cattle will not graze in infested areas.
Controlled in early stages by phenoxy compounds, relatively resistent to soil herbicides, pyrazon and trifluralin are effective.
Biological control in the USA with the beetles *Microlarinus lareynii* and *M. lypriformis*.

Zygophyllaceae

Literature

Bedevian, A. K., 1939: Illustrated Polyglottic Dictionary of Plant Names, Argus & Papazian Presses Cairo

Behboodi, E.: Weeds and Weed Control, Ministry of Agriculture Tehran, Bulletin Nr. 2

Davis, P. H., 1965: Flora of Turkey and the East Aegean Islands, Edinburgh University Press

Edgecombe, W. S., 1970: Weeds of Lebanon, American University of Beirut

Hegi, G., 1957: Illustrierte Flora von Mitteleuropa, Hauser Verlag München

Ivens, G. W., 1971: East African Weeds and Their Control, Oxford University Press

Kurhan, N. G.: Türkiye-nin Başlıca Yabancıotları ve Zararlı Oldukları Önemli Kültür Bitkileri Sözlüğü, Yabancıot Lâboratuvarı Şefi Zirai Mücadele Enstitüsü Ankara, Teknik Bülten No. 45

Polunin, O. and A. Huxley, 1968: Blumen am Mittelmeer, BLV München

Post, G. E., 1932: Flora of Syria, Palestine and Sinai, American University of Beirut

Quezel, P. and S. Santa, 1962: Nouvelle Flore de L'Algérie et des Régions Desertiques Méridionales, Centre National de la Recherche Scientifique Paris

Rechinger, K. H., 1964: Flora Iranica, Akademische Druck- und Verlagsanstalt Graz

Täckholm, V., 1956: Students' Flora of Egypt, Anglo-Egyptian Bookshop Cairo

Index

Latin plant names

Abutilon avicennae Gaertn.   160
Abutilon teophrastii Med.   160
Acacia stephaniana Willd.   148
Achillea santolina L.   34
Acroptilon picris (Pall.) DC.   36
Acroptilon repens (L.) DC.   36
Aegilops crassa Boiss.   98
Aegilops echinata Presl.   98
Aegilops elongata Lam.   98
Aegilops ovata L.   98
Aegilops triuncialis L.   98
Aethusa ammi Sprengel   200
Agrostemma githago L.   20
Agrostemma gracile Boiss.   20
Alhagi camelorum Fisch.   130
Alhagi persarum Boiss. et Buhse   130
Alhagi pseudalhagi (Bieb.) Desv.   130
Alternanthera achyranthes Forsk.   10
Alternanthera nodiflora R. Br.   10
Alternanthera sessilis (L.) R. Br.   10
Amaranthus blitoides S. Wats.   12
Amaranthus chlorostachys Willd.   14
Amaranthus retroflexus L.   14
Ammannia aegyptiaca Willd.   158
Ammania baccifera L.   158
Ammania senegalensis Lam.   158
Ammi baeberi Hoeq.   200
Ammi boeberi Hoekert   200
Ammi broussonetii DC.   200
Ammi cicutifolium Willd.   200
Ammi elatum Salisb.   200
Ammi maius L.   200
Ammi visnaga (L.) Lam.   200
Anacyclus clavatus Pers.   38
Anagallis arvensis L.   184
Anagallis monelli L.   184
Andropogon arundinaceum Scop.   128
Andropogon halepensis Brot.   128
Andropogon avenaceus Humb. et Kunth   128
Anthemis chia L.   38

Antirrhinum triphyllum L.   194
Aphaca marmorata Alef.   138
Aphaca vulgaris Alef.   138
Aphaca vulgaris Presl   138
Apium ammi Crantz   200
Apium ammi maius Crantz   200
Arabis sophia Bernh.   74
Arnoglossum lanceolatum (L.) S. F. Gray   178
Astoma seselifolium DC.   202
Avena barbata Pott   100, 102
Avena fatua L.   100, 102
Avena nigra Wallr.   100
Avena sterilis L.   100, 102
— spp. ludoviciana (Dur.) Gill. et Magne   102
— ssp. macrocarpa (Moench) Briquet   102
Avena syriaca Boiss. et BL. MS.   102
Brachiaria eruciformis (Sibth. et Sm.) Griseb.   104
Brachiaria isachne Stapf   104
Brassica campestris L. var. rapa Hartm.   70
Brassica eruca L.   76
Brassica orientalis L.   72
Brassica rapa L.   70
Bromus temulentus Bernh.   116
Caenotus canadensis (L.) Raf.   48
Calendula aegyptiaca Desf.   40
Calendula arvensis L.   40
Campanula syriaca Willd.   18
Capriola dactylon Kunze   108
Cardaria cochlearia Spach   78
Cardaria draba (L.) Desv.   78
Cardiolepis dentata Wallr.   78
Carduus marianus L.   56
Carduus syriacus L.   54
Caucalis strigosa Russ.   204
Caulis eruca E. H. L. Krause   76
Centaurea cyanoides Berger. et Wahlenb.   42
Centaurea cyanus L.   42

Centaurea picris Pall. 36
Centaurea repens L. 36
Cephalaria boissieri Reuter 92
Cephalaria syriaca (L.) Schrad. 92
Cerastium dichotomum L. 22
Chaerophyllum pecten-veneris Crantz 206
Chaerophyllum rostratum Lam. 206
Chaetochloa glauca Nash 122
Chaetochloa verticillata Nash 124
Chaetochloa viridis Nash 126
Chenopodium album L. 30
Chenopodium hybridum L. 30
Chenopodium murale L. 30
Chenopodium polyspermum L. 30
Chlorocyperus rotundus Palla 90
Chondrilla juncea L. 44
Chrozophora tinctoria (L.) Raf. 94
Chrysanthemum coronarium L. 46
Chrysanthemum segetum L. 46
Cirsium syriacum Gaertn. 54
Clymenum ochrus Alef. 142
Cnicus syriacus Roth 54
Cochlearia draba L. 78
Coix lacryma-jobi L. 106
Conringia orientalis (L.) Dum. 72
Conringia perfoliata Link 72
Convolvulus arvensis L. 64
Convolvulus deserti Hochst. et St. 66
Convolvulus minor Gilib. 64
Convolvulus pilosellifolius Desr. 66
Convolvulus sepium L. 64
Conyza canadensis (L.) Cronqu. 48
Coronilla scorpioides (L.) Koch 132
Craepalia temulenta Schrank 116
Croton tinctoria L. 94
Crucifera cardaria E. H. L. Krause 78
Crucifera eruca E. H. L. Krause 76
Cucubalus aegyptiaca L. 24
Cuscuta approximata Bab. 68
Cuscuta planiflora Ten. 68
— ssp. approximata (Bab.) Engelm. 68
Cynodon dactylon (L.) Pers. 108
Cyperus esculentus L. 90
Cyperus olivaris Targ.-Tozz. 90
Cyperus rotundus L. 90
Dactylon sanguinale Vill. 110
Datura metel L. 196
Datura stramonium L. 196

Descurea sophia Schur 74
Descurainia sophia Webb. 74
Digitaria sanguinalis Scop. 110
Echinochloa colonum (L.) Link 112
Echinochloa crus-galli (L.) Beauv. 112
Echinochloa eruciforme Reichb. 104
Emex spinosus (L.) Campd. 180
Eragrostis barrelieri Dav. 114
Eragrostis cilianensis (All.) Vign.-Lut. 114
Eragrostis minor Host 114
Eragrostis poaeformis Link 114
Eragrostis poaeoides Beauv. 114
Erigeron canadensis L. 48
Erigeron crispus Pourr. 48
Eruca cappadocica Reut. 76
Eruca eruca Asch. et Graebn. 76
Eruca foetida Moench 76
Eruca glabrescens Jord. 76
Eruca grandiflora Cav. 76
Eruca oleracea St.-Hil. 76
Eruca rucchetta Spach 76
Eurca sativa (Hill.) Gars. 76
Eruca sativa Mill. 76
Eruca silvestris Bub. 76
Eruca vesicaria ssp. sativa Thell. 76
Erysimum orientalis Mill. 72
Erysimum perfoliatum Crantz 72
Euphorbia canescens L. 96
Euphorbia chamaesyce L. 96
Euzomum sativum Link. 76
Fumaria officinalis L. 174
Galium aparine L. 190
Galium saccharatum All. 190
Galium tricorne Stokes 190
Galium tricornutum Dandy 190
Githago segetum Link 20
Glycyrrhiza glabra L. 134, 136
Glycyrrhiza glandulifera Waldst. et Kit. 134
Goebelia alopecuroides L. 136
Gomphrena sessilis L. 10
Gypsophila vaccaria Sibth. et Sm. 28
Hedysarum pseudalhagi Bieb. 130
Heliotropium dolosum de Not. 16
Heliotropium europaeum L. 16
Hesperis africana L. 80
Hibiscus trionum L. 162
Holcus exiguus Forsk. 128

Holcus halepensis L.   128
Hoplismenus crus-galli Dum.   112
Hultemia berberifolia Pall.   188
Hultemia persica (Gmel.) Bornm.   188
Hypechusa lutea Alef.   152
Illecebrum sesselis L.   10
Jundzillia draba Andrz.   78
Ketmia trionum Scop.   162
Kopsia ramosa (L.) Dum.   172
Lactuca orientalis Boiss.   50
Lactuca scariola L.   52
Lactuca serriola L.   52
Lactuca virosa L.   52
Lagonychium farctum (Banks et Sol.) Bobr.   148
Lagonychium stephanianum Bieb.   148
Lathraea phelipaea Forsk.   172
Lathyrus amphicarpos L.   140
Lathyrus aphaca L.   138
Lathyrus blepharicarpus Boiss.   140
Lathyrus cicera L.   140
Lathyrus currentifolius Lam.   142
Lathyrus dispermus Boiss.   138
Lathyrus marmoratus Boiss. et Bl.   140
Lathyrus ochrus DC.   142
Lathyrus polyanthus Boiss. et Bl.   138
Lathyrus segetum Lam.   138
Legousia falcata Fritsch   18
Legousia speculum-veneris (L.) Chaix   18
Lepidium draba L.   78
Lepidium drabifolium St. Lager   78
Leptilon canadensis (L.) Britt.   48
Linaria triphylla (L.) Mill.   194
Liquiritia officinalis Moench   134
Lisaea heterocarpa var. syriaca Post   204
Lisaea strigosa (Banks et Sol.) Eig.   204
Lisaea syriaca Boiss.   204
Lolium annuum Gilib.   116
Lolium multiflorum Lam.   116
Lolium perenne L.   116
Lolium temulentum L.   116
Lychnis githago Scop.   20
Malcolmia africana (L.) R. Br.   80
Malva neglecta Wallr.   164
Malva parviflora L.   164
Malva rotundifolia L.   164

Malva vulgaris Fries   164
Medicago denticulata Willd.   144
Medicago hispida Gaertn.   144
Medicago polymorpha Willd.   144
Melilotus albus Med.   146
Melilotus leucantha Koch   146
Melilotus melanosperma Besser   146
Melilotus rugosus Gilib.   146
Melilotus rugulosa Willd.   146
Melilotus vulgaris Willd.   146
Mimosa farcta Banks et Sol.   148
Moricandia arvensis (L.) DC.   82
Myagrum monospermum Forsk.   88
Myagrum paniculatum L.   86
Myagrum perfoliatum L.   84
Myagrum rugosum L.   88
Myrrhis pecten-veneris All.   206
Nasturtium draba Crantz   78
Neslia apiculata Fisch. et May.   86
Neslia paniculata (L.) Boiss.   86
Neslia paniculata Desv.   86
Notobasis syriaca (L.) Cass.   54
Ochrus pallida Pers.   142
Ochrus uniflorus Moench   142
Ornithopus scorpioides L.   132
Orobanche aegyptiaca Pers.   166, 172
Orobanche brassicae Novopokr.   172
Orobanche cernua Loefl.   168
Orobanche crenata Forsk.   170
Orobanche cumana Wallr.   168
Orobanche hispanica Boiss.   168
Orobanche klugei Schmitz et Regel   170
Orobanche longiflora Pers.   166
Orobanche mutelii F. W. Schultz   172
Orobanche pelargonii Caldesi   170
Orobanche picta Wilms   170
Orobanche pruinosa Lapeyr.   170
Orobanche ramosa L.   166
Orobanche segetum Spruner   170
Orobanche speciosa DC. et Lam.   170
Orobus aphaca Döll   138
Panicum crus-corvi L.   112
Panicum crus-galli L.   112
Panicum dactylon L.   108
Panicum eruciforme Sibth. et Sm.   104
Panicum glaucum L.   122
Panicum isachne Roth   104
Panicum sanguinale L.   110
Panicum verticillatum L.   124

Panicum viride L.   126
Pecten veneris Lam.   206
Pectinaria vulgaris Bernh.   206
Peganum harmala L.   208
Pennisetum glaucum R. Br.   122
Phalaris brachystachys Link   118, 120
Phalaris minor Retz.   118, 120
Phalaris paradoxa L.   118, 120
Phalaris quadrivalvis Lag   118
Phalaris velutina Forsk.   110
Phelipaea aegyptiaca Walp.   166
Phelipaea mutelii Reuter   172
Phelipaea ramosa (L.) C. A. Mey.   172
Phenopus orientalis Boiss.   50
Phytolacca americana L.   176
Phytolacca decandra L.   176
Pisum ochrus L.   142
Plantago flexuosa Gaud.   178
Plantago lanceaefolia Salisb.   178
Plantago lanceolata L.   178
Plantago longistipes Royle   178
Plantago sylvatica Martius   178
Poa eragrostis L.   114
Portulaca oleracea L.   182
Prismatocarpus falcatus Ten.   18
Prosopis farcta (Banks et Sol.) Macbride   148
Prosopis stephaniana (Willd.) Kunth   148
Pycreus rotundus Hayek   90
Ranunculus arvensis L.   186
Ranunculus repens L.   186
Raphanus eruca Crantz   76
Rapistrum perenne (L.) All.   88
Rapistrum rugosum (L.) All.   88
Rhicinoides tinctoria Moench   94
Rosa persica J. F. Gmel.   188
Rosa simplicifolia Salisb.   188
Rubia peregrina L.   192
Rubia tinctorum L.   192
Rumex glaber Forsk.   180
Rumex spinosus L.   180
Salsola kali L.   32
Saponaria hispanica Mill.   28
Saponaria perfoliata (Gilib.) Hal.   28
Saponaria segetalis Neck.   28
Saponaria vaccaria L.   28
Scabiosa syriaca L.   92
Scaligera cretica Boiss.   202
Scandix cornuta Gilib.   206
Scandix iberica Bieb.   206
Scandix pecten Scop.   206
Scandix pecten-veneris L.   206
Scandix pectinifera Stokes   206
Scandix pectiniformis St. Lager   206
Scandix rostrata Salisb.   206
Scandix vulgaris S. F. Gray   206
Scorzonera buphthalmoides DC.   58
Scorpiurus minima A. Los.   150
Scorpiurus muricatus L. var. subvillosus (L.) Fiori   150
Scorpiurus subvillosa L.   150
Scorpiurus sulcata L.   150
Scorpiurus vermiculatus L.   150
Selinum ammoides E. H. L. Krause   200
Selinum ammoides E. H. Krause   200
Selinum pecten E. H. L. Krause   206
Setaria glauca (L.) Beauv.   122, 124, 126
Setaria lutescens (Weigel) F. T. Hubb.   122
Setaria pallidifusca Stapf   122
Setaria panicea Schinz et Thellg.   124
Setaria verticillata (L.) Beauv.   122, 124, 126
Setaria viridis (L.) Beauv.   122, 124, 126
Sida abutilon L.   160
Sida tiliifolia Fischer   160
Silene aegyptiaca (L.) L. f.   24
Silene atocion Juss.   24
Silene conoidea L.   26
Silene orchidea L.   24
Silene rubella L.   24
Silybum marianum (L.) Gaertn.   56
Sinapis eruca Clairv.   76
Sison maior Eaton et Wright   200
Sisymbrium parviflora Lam.   74
Sisymbrium sophia L.   74
Sisymbrium tripinnatum DC.   74
Solanum alatum Moench   198
Solanum judaicum Bess.   198
Solanum nigrum L.   198
Sophia vulgaris Fourn.   74
Sorghum halepense (L.) Pers.   128
Specularia falcata (Ren.) A. DC.   18
Stramonium spinosum Lam.   196
Syntherisma vulgare Schrad.   110
Telanthera amoena Regel   10
Tournesolia tinctoria Baill.   94
Trachypogon avenaceus Nees   128

Tragopogon buphthalmoides (DC.) Boiss. 58	190	بَقراخ
Tribulus longipetalus Viv. 210	164	بَنيرَك
Tribulus mollis Ehrenb. 210		
Tribulus terrestris L. 210	196	تاقُرِز
Trionum diffusum Moench 162		
Triticum triunciale Gren. et Godr. 98	198	تامريزى
Vaccaria hispanica (Mill.) Rausch. 28		
Vaccaria parviflora Moench 28	38	تافندست
Vaccaria pyramidata Med. 28		
Vaccaria segetalis (Neck.) Garcke 28	180	ترب كوهى
Valantia triflora Lam. 190		
Vicia angustifolia Grufb. 154	136	تلخ بيان
Vicia communis Rouy 154		
Vicia cracca L. 156	36	تلخه
Vicia lutea L. 152		
Vicia sativa L. 154	62	تون
Vicia varia Host 156		
Vicia villosa Roth 156	28	جغجغك
Visnaga vulgaris Bubani 200		
Vogelia apiculata (F. et M.) Vierh. 86	100	جودوسر
Vogelia paniculata (L.) Hornem. 86		
Vogelia sagittata Med. 86	104	چپ واش
Wiggersia lutea Gaertn. 152		
Wilckia africana Halacs. 80	210	خارخسك
Wylia pecten-veneris Bubani 206		
Xanthium brasilicum Vell. 62	130	خارشتر
Xanthium echinatum Murr. 62		
Xanthium spinosum L. 60, 62		
Xanthium strumarium L. 62	74	خاكشير
	182	خرفه
Iranian plant names		
	138	خُلَر
126	ارزن وحشى	
	142	خَلَر
78	ازمک	
	160	دوكنف
122	اسب واش	
	68	سس
208	اسفند	
	92	سرشكافته
90	اويارسلام	
	30	سلمه تره
178	بارهنگ	
	112	سوروف
118	بذرك كاناري	
	174	شاتره
184	بذرك وحشى	
	106	شال تسبيح

50	شيرشى		Arabian plant names
96	شبرك		
32	شورد	178	إدهام الكبش
116	علكن	32	اشنان
120	غلارس	40	الجنوه
44	قندروند	150	العقربان
128	ميان	24	أهوان
148	جغجغه	72	بجبج
52	صماجاقن،	38	نافذ مست
110	ممادرس	162	تيل شبلاني
42	ملّ شم	76	جرجير
158	كورجين اباتى	88	حارة
94	كوش برو	48	حشيشة الجن
64	لبلاب	128	حشيشة الفرس
156	ماشك	138	حمام البرج
154	ماشف	68	حسول
134	منكو	146	حنزقوق
108	مرغ	164	خبيزة برى
76	منداب	52	خه البحر
188	ورك	200	خه شبلانيه
200	وابه	196	دانوره
40	هيت بهاروشى	190	ذبين
102	يرلاك	110	زنبره
146	يونجه زرد	210	دفن الشيخ
144	يونجه وحى	112	دنيبه
		210	ذبل النار

58	ذنب الفرس	192	توه	
158	رجل حمامة	124	فح النار	
182	رجله	78	قنبره	
30	ركب الجمل	82	كرنب بري	
186	زغنته	174	كسفارة الحمار	
116	زوان	96	لبن	
90	سعد	42	مرايز	
202	سمرة	206	مثل الرامي	
70	شولجم	152	بحره	
62	شبط	108	نجيل	
60	شبط	86	نسية	
122	شمر النار	144	نفل	
148	ششدوي	94	نيلي	
74	شبث	154	هالوك	
56	شوك الجمل	208	هرس	
92	طردان	44	هندباء بري	
180	طرس العجوز	50	ياخن	
130	عقول			
64	عليه			
198	عنب الديب			
176	عنب أمريكي	Turkish plant names		
160	عوس الغنم			
184	عين الجمل	Acımık 36		
54	غرفت الجمل	Ak hindiba 44		
28	فول العرب	Ak kaz ayağı 30		
		Ak pazı 30		
		Akrep otu 16		

Aktaş yoncası 146
Arap baklası 28
Arnavut darısı 124
Ayni sefa 40
Bahçe hardalı 76
Bambul otu 94
Beyaz çiçekli canavar otu 170
Boya otu 94
Buğday karamuğu 20
Burgulu fasulye 148
Cavers otu 110
Cüce yabani ebe gömeci 164
Çatal otu 110
Çeti 148
Çoban tarağı 206
Çok senelik yabani tere 78
Dağındest 38
Darıcan 112
Darı otu 110
Dar yapraklı sinir otu 178
Delice 116
Deli yulaf 100
Demir dikeni 210
Deve dikeni 130
Dikenli soda otu 32
Dineba 112
Doğu koringyası 72
Düğün 186
Fuvve 192
Gazel lokması 10
Gönül hardalı 84
Gözyaşı otu 106
Güvercin ayağı 158
Hind keneviri 160
Horoz kuyruğu 14
İt üzümü 198
Kaba yonca 144
Kanyaş 128
Karaman kimyonu 200
Kekre 36
Kirpi darı 124
Kir teresi 78
Kısır yulaf 102
Kıssa ebegümeci 164
Kızıl boya 192
Kök boyası 192
Köpek dişi ayrığı 108
Köpek memesi 198

Köpek üzümü 198
Köşeli yapraklı 190
Krizantem 46
Küçük daneli kuş yemi 120
Küçük turp 88
Mahmur 208
Mariam anna dikeni 56
Mavi çiçekli canavar otu 172
Mavi peygamber çiçeği 42
Meyan kökü 134
Meyan otu 134
Mürdümük 138
Orun 92
Pelemir 92
Pirinç otu 112
Portakal nerkizi 40
Sakalotu 98
Sari tüylü darı 122
Semiz otu 182
Servi otu 34
Sıçan saçı 122
Sıraca otu 62
Sütlüğen 96
Şahtere 174
Şalgam 70
Şeceri boyası otu 176
Şeytan elması 196
Şeytan keneviri 162
Şifa otu 48
Tarla farekulağı 184
Tarla sarmasağı 64
Tavşan bezelyesi 138
Topalak 90
Ufak çayır güzeli 114
Uskurçina 58
Uzun süpürge otu 74
Üzerlik otu 208
Yabani lahana 82
Yabani salata 52
Yağ marulu 52
Yemlik 20
Yeşil cin darı 126
Yeşil tüylü darı 126
Yoğurt otu 190
Yonka küskütü 68
Zincir bıtrağı 60
Zivan 92, 116
Zühre tarağı 206

English plant names

African rue 208
American velvet leaf 160
Animated oats 102
Astoma 202
Ball mustard 86
Barnyard grass 112
Bermuda grass 108
Black nightshade 198
Bladder hibiscus 162
Branched broomrape 172
Bristly foxtail 124
Bulls-eye 58
Bur clover 144
Cabbage-flowered moricandia 82
Camelthorn 130
Cocklebur 62
Common bishop's weed 200
Common fumitory 174
Common liquorice 134
Common purslane 182
Common turnip 70
Common vetch 154
Compass plant 52
Conoid catchfly 26
Corn cockle 20
Corn crowfoot 186
Coronilla 132
Cowherb 28
Crabgrass 110
Crenated spurge 96
Crown daisy 46
Darnel 116
Dodder 68
Drooping broomrape 168
Dwarf mallow 164
Dyers madder 192
Egyptian broomrape 166
Egyptian catchfly 24
European heliotrope 16
European turnsole 16
Field bindweed 64
Field marigold 40
Flixweed 74
Flower of an hour 162
Forked mouse-ear 22
Furrowed caterpillar 150

Garden rocket 76
Goatsbeard 58
Gold of pleasure 84
Great bur parsley 204
Great wild oat 102
Green bristlegrass 126
Green foxtail 126
Gum succory 44
Hares ear 72
Hoary cress 78
Horseweed 48
Jimson weed 196
Jobs tears 106
Johnson grass 128
Ladys-thistle 56
Lamb's quarters 30
Lesser canary grass 120
Longwort 38
Mat amaranth 12
Narrow-leaved plantain 178
Nutgrass 90
Officinal croton 94
Oriental lettuce 50
Perennial peppergrass 78
Pigeon-berry 176
Pigweed 14
Pimpernel 184
Pink cockle 28
Prickly dock 180
Prickly lettuce 52
Puncture vine 210
Redroot 14
Ribgrass 178
Rough-podded vetch 152
Rough bedstraw 190
Russian knapweed 36
Russian thistle 32
Santolina milfoil 34
Scalloped broomrape 170
Sessile-flowered globe amaranth 10
Shepherds needle 206
Short-spiked canary grass 118
Signal grass 104
Skeleton weed 44
Spiny cocklebur 60
Spreading love grass 114
Spreading pigweed 12
Sweet melilot 146

Syrian cornflower 42
Syrian cephalaria 92
Syrian plumed thistle 54
Syrian scabious 92
Syrian venus'-looking-glass 18
Thorn apple 196
Three-inch goats face grass 98
Three-leaved toadflax 194
Tooth cup 158
Virginian poke 176
White melilot 146
Wild oat 100
Wing-podded vetchling 140
Winter vetch 156
Wrinkled gold-of-pleasure 88
Yellow bristlegrass 122
Yellow foxtail 122
Yellow pea 142
Yellow vetch 152
Yellow vetchling 138

French plant names

Abutilon ordinaire 160
Achillée santolin 34
Alpiste 118
Amarante fausse blette 12
Amarante reflechie 14
Ammannie 158
Anacycle 38
Ansérine 30
Avoine stérile 102
Belle Orobanche 170
Bleuet 42
Brède chevrette 10
Centaurée aux amères 36
Céphalarie 92
Céraiste inflate 22
Chameau-sainfoin 130
Chardon de Syrie 54
Chardon-Marie 56
Chenillette 150
Chenopode blanc 30
Chiendent dactyle 108

Chiendent à pied de poule 108
Chou-rave 70
Chrysanthéme des couronnes 46
Croix de Malte 210
Croton des teinturiers 94
Cuscute 68
Digitaire sanguinale 110
Egilops 98
Emex épineux 180
Eragrostis amourette 114
Erigéron du Canada 48
Euphorbe 96
Folle Avoine 100
Fumeterre 174
Gaillet à trois corne 190
Garance sauvage 192
Gesse 140
Gesse aphaca 138
Gesse ochre 142
Grand Ajoua 200
Guimauve jaune 160
Héliotrop d'Europe 16
Herbe de Ste. Sophie 74
Ivraie 116
Ketmie d'Afrique 162
Laitue orientale 50
Laitue scarole 52
Lampourde épineuse 60
Lampourde strumarium 62
Larmilles 106
Linaire 194
Liseron des champs 64
Luzerne hispide 144
Mauve des chemins 164
Mélilot blanc 146
Morelle noire 198
Moricandie des champs 82
Mouron des champs 184
Myagrum perfolie 84
Neslie paniculée 86
Nielle des blés 20
Ocre 142
Oreille de lièvre 178
Orobanche blanc 170
Orobanche du chanvre 172
Pain blanc 78
Passerage 78
Peigne de Vénus 206

Petit Phalaris   120
Pied de coq   112
Plantain   178
Pomme épineuse   196
Pourpier potager   182
Queue de Renard   14
Queue de Scorpion   132
Raisin d'Amerique   176
Rapistre   88
Réglisse glabre   134
Renoncule des champs   186
Roquette   76
Roquette d'Orient   72
Rue sauvage   208
Salsifis   58

Saponaire des vaches   28
Scorpiure   150
Setaire glauque   122
Setaire verte   126
Setaire verticillée   124
Silene conique   26
Sisymbre Sophia   74
Sorgho d'Alep   128
Souchet à tubercules   90
Souci d'Algérie   40
Soude kali   32
Spéculaire   18
Vesce commune   154
Vesce jaune   152
Vesce velue   156

SCHRIFTEN-REIHE DER GTZ

Die Schriftenreihe der GTZ will vor allem

die nationale und internationale Fachöffentlichkeit über Erfahrungen und Arbeitsergebnisse, die im Rahmen der Technischen Zusammenarbeit mit Entwicklungsländern gesammelt wurden, unterrichten;

bei der projektbegleitenden Öffentlichkeitsarbeit mitwirken;

den fachlichen Informationsaustausch der in Projekten der Technischen Zusammenarbeit tätigen deutschen und einheimischen Fachkräfte unterstützen.

Bisher wurden in dieser Schriftenreihe folgende Themen publiziert: [1])

---

[1]) Genannt sind jeweils die Originaltitel. In Klammern ist die entsprechende deutsche Übersetzung angegeben.

1
Gachet, Paul und Jaritz, Günther:
„Situation und Perspektiven der Futterproduktion im Trockenanbau in Nordtunesien". 1972. 30 Seiten. DM 5,–

2
Jahn und König:
„Forst in Paktia/Afghanistan". 1972. 56 Seiten. Dreisprachig (Englisch, Farsi, Deutsch). DM 5,—

3
Jaritz, Günther:
„Die Weidewirtschaft im australischen Winterregenklima und ihre Bedeutung für die Entwicklung der Landwirtschaft in den nordafrikanischen Maghrebländern". 1973. 40 Seiten. DM 5,–

4
Wienberg, Dieter; Weiler, Norbert und Seidel, Helmut:
„Der Erdbeeranbau in Spanien". 1972. 92 Seiten. DM 5,–

5
„Beiträge deutscher Forschungsstätten zur Agrarentwicklung in der Dritten Welt". 1973. 568 Seiten. DM 5,–

6
„Deutsche Agrarhilfe – was, wo, wie? 1973". 2. Auflage. 1973. 600 Seiten. DM 5,–

7
Seidel, Helmut und Wienberg, Dieter:
„Gemüsesortenversuche in Südspanien". 1973. 102 Seiten. DM 5,–

8
„Tsetse- und Trypanosomiasisbekämpfung". 1973. 102 Seiten. DM 5,–

9
Schieber, Eugenio:
„Informe Sobre Algunos Estudios Fitopatologicos Efectuados en la República Dominicana" (Bericht über einige phytopathologische Studien in der Dominikanischen Republik). 1973. 66 Seiten, 35 Abbildungen. DM 5,–

10
Bautista, Juan Elias; Hansen del Orbe, Raymundo und Jürgens, Gerhard:
„Control de Malezas en la República Dominicana" (Unkrautbekämpfung in der Dominikanischen Republik). 1973. 40 Seiten. DM 5,–

11
„Internationale Agrarentwicklung zwischen Theorie und Praxis". 1974. 390 Seiten. DM 5,–

12
Adelhelm, Rainer und Steck, Karl:
„Agricultural Mechanisation – Costs and Profitability" (Mechanisierung der Landwirtschaft – Kosten und Rentabilität). 1974. 70 Seiten. DM 5,–

13
Hübl, Klaus; Huhn und Kröger, Knud:
„Mokwa Cattle Ranch". 1974. 44 Seiten. Dreisprachig (Englisch, Französisch, Deutsch). DM 5,–

14
„La Lutte contre la Mouche Tse-Tse et la Trypanosomiase" (Fachgespräch über Trypanosomiasis und Tsetsebekämpfung). 1974. 106 Seiten. DM 5,–

15
Zeuner, Tim:
„Mandi – Projekt in einer indischen Bergregion". 1974. 76 Seiten. 1 Karte. 41 Abbildungen. Zweisprachig (Englisch und Deutsch). DM 5,–

16
Rüchel, Werner-Michael:
„Chemoprophylaxe der bovinen Trypanosomiasis". 1974. 232 Seiten. DM 5,–

17
Lindau, Manfred:
„El Koudia/Marokko – Futterbau und Tierhaltung – Culture fourragére et entretien du bétail". 1974. 74 Seiten. DM 5,–

18
Kopp, Erwin:
„Das Produktionspotential des semiariden tunesischen Oberen Medjerdatales bei Beregnung". 1975. 322 Seiten. DM 5,–

19
Grove, Dietrich:
„Ambulante andrologische Diagnostik am Rind in warmen Ländern". 1975. 288 Seiten. 40 Abbildungen. DM 5,−

20
Eisenhauer, Georg (Redaktion):
„Forstliche Fakultät Valdivia/Chile − Facultad de Ingenieria Forestal Valdivia/Chile". 1975. 245 Seiten. DM 5,−

21
Burgemeister, Rainer:
„Elévage de Chameaux en Afrique du Nord" (Kamelzucht in Nordafrika). 1975. 85 Seiten. DM 5,−

22
Agpaoa, A.; Endagan, D.; Festin, S.; Gumayagay, J.; Hoenninger, Th.; Seeber, G.; Unkel, K. und Weidelt, H. J.:
„Manual of Reforestation and Erosion Control for the Philippines" (Handbuch der Aufforstung und Erosionskontrolle auf den Philippinen). 1975. 569 Seiten. DM 5,−

23
Jürgens, Gerhard (Redaktion):
„Curso Basico sobre Control de Malezas en la República Dominicana" (Grundkurs zur Unkrautbekämpfung in der Dominikanischen Republik). 1975. 173 Seiten. DM 5,−

24
Schieber, Eugenio:
„El Status Presente de la Herrumbre del Café en America del Sur" (Der aktuelle Stand der Kaffeerostbekämpfung in Südamerika). 1975. 22 Seiten. DM 5,−

25
Rohrmoser, Klaus:
„Ölpflanzenzüchtung in Marokko − Selection des Oleagineux au Maroc". 1975. 278 Seiten. 8 Colorfotos, 1 Übersichtskarte. Zweisprachig (Deutsch und Französisch). DM 5,−

26
Bonarius, Helmut:
„Physical Properties of Soils in the Kilombero Valley/Tanzania" (Physikalische Zusammensetzung der Böden im Kilombero-Tal/Tansania). 1975. 34 Seiten. DM 5,−

27
„Mandi – A Project in a Mountainous Region of India" (Mandi-Projekt in einer indischen Bergregion). 1975. (Englisch/Hindi). 13 Seiten. DM 5,–

28
Schmidt, G. und Hesse, F.-W.:
„Einführung der Zuckerrübe in Marokko – Introduction de la betterave sucriére au Maroc". 1975. 136 Seiten. 16 Tabellen. 17 Schwarzweißfotos. Mehrfarbige Standortkarte. Zweisprachig (Deutsch und Französisch. DM 8,–

29
„Landwirtschaftliche Entwicklung in West-Sumatra" 1976. 30 Seiten. 13 Schwarzweißfotos, 1 farbige Standortkarte. DM 5,–

30
Rüchel, Werner-Michael:
„Chemoprophylaxis of Bovine Trypanosomiasis" (Chemoprophylaxe der bovinen Trypanosomiasis). 1975. 252 Seiten. DM 5,–

31
„Bildung und Wissenschaft in Entwicklungsländern" – Die Maßnahmen der staatlichen deutschen Bildungs- und Wissenschaftsförderung. 1976. 242 Seiten. DM 13,50

32
Wagener, Wilhelm E.:
„Baukasten für die praktisch-pädagogische Counterpartausbildung". 1976. 156 Seiten. DM 18,50

33
„Journées Agrostologie – Elévage des Ruminants". (Erfahrungsaustausch über Weideverbesserung). 1976. 188 Seiten. DM 5,–

34
„Internationale Zusammenarbeit im Agrarbereich – was, wo, wie?". 3. Auflage. 1976. 542 Seiten. DM 16,50

35
„Bessere Ernten für Minas Gerais". Dreisprachige PR-Broschüre (Portugiesisch, Englisch, Deutsch).

36
„La Défence des Cultures en Tunisie – en considérant particuliérement la Tunisie et le Maroc" (Pflanzenschutz in Nordafrika unter besonderer Berücksichtigung von Tunesien und Marokko). 1976. 272 Seiten. 375 Abbildungen. DM 41,20

37
„Agricultural Development in West Sumatra" (Landwirtschaftliche Entwicklung in West-Sumatra). 1976. 30 Seiten. 13 Schwarzweißfotos. 1 farbige Standortkarte. DM 5,–

38
Kopp, Erwin:
Le Potentiel de Production dans la Regiôn semiaride de la Haute Vallée de la Medjerda tunisienne sous irrigation par aspersion" (Französischsprachige Ausgabe der Nummer 18). 1977. 360 Seiten. DM 26,–

39
Schmutterer, Heinz:
„Plagas e Enfermedades de Algodon en Centro America" (Krankheiten und Schädlinge bei Baumwolle in Zentralamerika). 1977. 104 Seiten. 50 Colorabbildungen. DM 22,–

40
„Dritte externe Veterinärtagung". 1977. 370 Seiten. DM 24,50

41
Becker, Günther:
„Holzzerstörung durch Termiten im Zentralafrikanischen Kaiserreich – Destruction du bois par les termites dans l'Empire Centrafricain". 1977. 96 Seiten. Zweisprachige Publikation (Deutsch und Französisch).

42
Furtmayr, Ludwig:
„Besamungsstationen an tropischen und subtropischen Standorten". 1977. 64 Seiten.

43
„Parfumpflanzenanbau in Tunesien". 1977. Zweisprachige Publikation (Französisch und Deutsch).

44*
„Vikunjabewirtschaftung in Peru". 1977. Mehrsprachige Publikation.

45
Grove, Dietrich:
„Diagnostico Andrológico Ambulante en el Bovino en Paises Cálidos" (Spanische Übersetzung der Nummer 19). 1977.

46
Nägel, Ludwig:
„Aquakultur in der Dritten Welt". 1977. 110 Seiten.

47
Wagener, Wilhelm E.:
„Model for Practical-Educational Counterpart Training". 1977. 106 Seiten. DM 18.50

48
Metschies, Gerhard:
„Ländlicher Straßenbau in Entwicklungsländern". 1977. 218 Seiten. DM 25,–